# A Living Profit

### Studies in the Social History of
### Canadian Business, 1883-1911

Michael Bliss

McClelland and Stewart Limited

The illustrations used in this
book originally appeared in
Grip and Industrial Canada

The Canadian Publishers
McClelland and Stewart Limited
25 Hollinger Road, Toronto

Printed and bound in Canada

The book has been published
with the help of a grant from the
Social Science Research Council of Canada, using funds provided by the Canada Council.

# Contents

For Elizabeth

# The Canadian Social History Series

Social history is about people. This series is concerned with broadening the understanding of Canadian history, widening it from a story of past politics to a portrayal of the context in which Canadians have lived and interreacted with one another.

The series takes the broadest possible view of the subject matter of social history. It is concerned not only to encompass as much of the sweep of Canadian history as possible, but also to exploit the whole range of scholarship in this country. That means that it is interested in the social history of our native peoples, in immigration and acculturation, in the development of social institutions such as the family, classes, and voluntary organizations, in ideas and attitudes in their social context, in the social dimension of occupations and industries, in community formation and urban growth, in social movements such as the temperance crusade, the movement for prison reform, and that for the liberation of women, in sports and leisure activities. Social history is the history of the full range of human life, and this series will attempt to represent that range.

Canadian social history is still in its infancy. In few of the areas mentioned above has scholarship developed to the point at which a monograph covering any one of them for the whole time-span could be written. This series, therefore, proposes to take advantage of the work being done on specialized areas and fairly brief chronological periods. Without being narrow, the volumes will present in-depth studies of major themes, rather than sweeping generalities over the whole of Canadian history. Obviously it is hoped that, eventually, the series will build to a comprehensive social history of Canada; in the meantime, the individual volumes will be exemplary of both the subject matter and the approaches of that social history.

Our aim is a series which will be of use both to general readers and to students of history. All of those interested in the development of this country will find excitement in these studies of the major themes of social history. At the same time, these are works of original scholarship, opening up new areas of Canadian history for students and academics. So, the books contain the documentation necessary to guide students to the key sources, but are not so weighed down with scholarly paraphernalia as to lose their clarity and readability. Canadians, whether or not they are scholars, are growing ever more concerned to discover their real history. We hope this series will contribute to that discovery.

S. F. Wise
Michael S. Cross

# Acknowledgements

Professor Ramsay Cook supervised the doctoral thesis for the University of Toronto on which this book is based. Without his generosity, tolerance and patience the thesis would never have been finished. Without his constant good advice and that of Professor Craig Brown it would have been much more inadequate than it is. In revising the thesis I have been particularly helped by the critical comments of Professors H. V. Nelles and Michael Cross, and by the continuing influence of Miss Evelyn G. Hicks.

Professor Kenneth McNaught's stimulating lectures in American history at the University of Toronto first interested me in the role of businessmen in society. An examination of what American businessmen thought, "or thought they thought," by E. C. Kirkland, entitled *Dream and Thought in the Business Community, 1860-1900,* was the direct inspiration of this study. The research was generously supported by two doctoral fellowships from the Canada Council. I am particularly indebted to the Canadian Manufacturers' Association and its officers for having given me complete access to its records for the years prior to 1915. The most helpful of the many librarians who assisted me was Mrs. Jean Mackay of Maclean-Hunter Limited, who allowed a bothersome outsider total freedom in the use of the company's superb library of business journals. Largely because of her interest in this work the Maclean-Hunter collection has since been donated to the University of Toronto.

My wife, Elizabeth, does not type my manuscripts. But in every other way she makes them possible.

Everything wrong with this book is my fault.

M.B.

# Introduction

This book is a collection of studies in the thought of Canadian businessmen during the formative years of modern Canadian society. The essays are an attempt to discover what was on the minds of businessmen, an exploration of the climate of opinion in the business community. This is not a specialized inquiry by an economic or business historian, and the studies do not treat such technical problems as the dynamics of economic development or the quality of Canadian entrepreneurship. Instead, as a general social historian, I have used the sources to examine one among many occupational groups in a larger society. The aim was simply to find out and report upon the most important and interesting ideas businessmen held in the years 1883 to 1911. The following six chapters are that report; the conclusion is a discussion of some of its implications.

Defining businessmen as the owners or operators of enterprises risking capital in the hope of profit, I have tried to explore the ideas of corner grocers and Western lumber dealers as well as those of railway presidents and textile magnates. The principal sources include trade journals catering to grocers and druggists, the leading Canadian financial papers, government inquiries, and the private papers of business associations and a few leading entrepreneurs. Because the aim has been to portray the corporate thought of the business community, no special groups of businessmen have been singled out for attention except as the sources and topics dictated.

One result of this method is that the following chapters often focus upon similarities rather than differences among businessmen. Most of the topics studied are those that were faced by most men in business regardless of the location, nature, and size of their operations. The problem of competition, for example, was no less real to a bank president in Montreal than it was to a dry goods man in Halifax or Edmonton. A master printer employing ten hands had to grapple with the labour question as earnestly as the textile mill manager employing a thousand. Changes in the tariff, though of life and death interest to the manufacturer, affected everyone engaged in business in Canada. Success in business was what everyone strove for and no man whose activity was directed at making a profit was immune from charges of money-grubbing and exploitation. These problems flowed out of situations encountered in business by all businessmen.

Moreover, with some stated exceptions, I have found that the response to such problems as competition, the rise of trade unions, the criticism of wealth, or the conflicting claims of other interest groups did not vary among businessmen according to what some think are traditional determinants of opinion – regional background, religious belief, education, or the specific nature of a man's business. The fact that a man was a businessman was more important in the formation of his attitudes, at least on the issues discussed here, than that he may have been a Methodist, Maritimer, French-Canadian, Roman Catholic, manufacturer, financier, public school drop-out, or university graduate. The relationship of religious background to business practice, to take one example, was once neatly disposed of by a correspondent to a trade journal that had criticized the business morals of Jews: "The Jew is tricky! Is he? Were you ever taken in by a Methodist class leader on a real estate trade? Did you ever get into close quarters with a Presbyterian speculator? Did you ever buy mining stock on the representations of an Episcopalian broker? Did you ever take a man's word any quicker because he was a Baptist or a Roman Catholic?"[1]

Another characteristic of these studies is that they tend to stress continuities in business thought over a thirty-year time span and in periods of depression and prosperity. The years 1883 to 1911 were chosen because, although they were obviously a period of massive change in Canadian economic life, it was also true that a number of important factors affecting the environment in which business was conducted remained constant. Taxation was always low; federal income and corporation taxes were yet to be enacted as emergency measures in the Great War. More than in any succeeding period, governments were generally friendly to private enterprise, combining generous subsidies with a minimum of social control of business and hedging the Canadian market with substantial protective tariffs. No one would have known the meaning of such terms as the welfare state or the mixed economy. Within business, the economy was already by the early 1880s equipped with sophisticated transportation, banking, and distribution facilities, while manufacturing was enjoying hothouse growth thanks to the National Policy tariff schedules first established in 1879. Joint-stock corporations with thousands of employees – the railways, banks, and a number of the new manufacturing enterprises – already existed side by side with family shops, partnerships, and private banks. Although the size of firms, the complexity of organizations, and reliance on outside financing would all substantially increase during the period, there were few Canadian organization men, specialists in management, or graduates of sophisticated business colleges before at least the 1920s. Most of the great finance capitalists who formed the Canadian plutocracy by 1911 and headed the multi-million dollar corporations created in the recent wave of mergers – Mackenzie and Mann, Herbert Holt, Frederic Nicholls, George Cox, E. R. Wood, James Ross, and others – had begun their careers as subcontractors and clerks a generation before. If anything, their astonishing success at business seemed to have verified and reinforced their belief in the simple business maxims developed early in their lives. The twenty-eight years of Canadian history covered in this study were, of course, roughly equivalent to the active business life of one generation.

It was a generation in which the course of business could vary from black depression to boundless expansion. One still common interpretation of the economic history of the period emphasizes radical discontinuity, the contrast between the anxieties of the supposed depression of the 1880s and 1890s and the great days of the "Laurier boom" when the twentieth century seemed to belong to Canadians in general and Canadian businessmen in particular. More recent scholarship has led to a reconsideration of the Canadian rate of growth before 1896, and considerable doubt has been cast on the older notions of a sustained depression lasting until about 1896 followed by a Rostowian "take-off" into industrialization. It now seems clear that both the manufacturing and financial sectors enjoyed very substantial growth through most of the "great depression" of the late nineteenth century. If O. J. Firestone's estimates of gross national product are accurate, the general growth rate in the economy of 4 per cent per annum between 1873 and 1896, despite more rapid American progress, is still impressive. Furthermore, as P. B. Waite has noted, the incidence of booms and depressions was always uneven: some firms and industries prospered through the worst of times; and, of course, there were businessmen in trouble during the best of times after 1900. As G. W. Bertram has suggested, it seems most appropriate to view the whole period as one of steady movement towards industrialization, "not marked by identifiable discontinuities."[2]

One final element linking the decades was the continuity of many

11

of the problems affecting businessmen. Realistically, trade unions were not a significant threat to business well-being in Canada until at least 1918-1919; yet the incidence of bitter industrial warfare in other countries in the 1870s and 1880s, combined with the revival of indigenous Canadian craft unionism and the spread of the Knights of Labor in the mid-1880s, caused Canadian businessmen to consider and debate the "menace" of organized labour at least as vigorously in that decade as they would thirty years later. It was probably only with the merger movement of 1909-1912 that monopolies and oligopolies became economically important in Canadian life; in the late 1880s, though, the widespread discussion of the problem of competition and combination established attitudes from which there would be no significant variation in the next generation. When Mackenzie King introduced his Combines Investigation Act in 1910 he used the 1888 investigation of combines as his basic piece of evidence; the main opposition to his new legislation came from the same leaders of the same combine, the Dominion Wholesale Grocers' Guild, that had been at the centre of the earlier investigation. Throughout the period, the National Policy tariff was the single most important political issue in the country. The 1911 election was a re-run of 1891, complete with the same flag-waving opposition to reciprocity, the same charges of veiled treason, and the same intervention by Sir William Van Horne and the Canadian Manufacturers' Association. In the early 1880s businessmen complained that professional politicians paid too much attention to farmers and trade unions; by 1911 they were sure that the situation had worsened. Through all these years businessmen and business editors (who, as the Note on Sources discusses, seem to have accurately reflected the views of their constituents) spoke their minds on questions of the day with a candour, sometimes bordering on naivité, that would become unusual in a later generation dominated by professional public relations specialists.

Most discussions of the role of businessmen in Canadian society at the time and since have been variations on two common views of business enterprise. To many, probably most, Canadians before the social disruption of 1914-1918, the country's business leaders were captains of industry; they were the men who were building a nation by driving steel through the wilderness, raising the tall chimneys of thriving manufactories, blasting metals out of the Canadian Shield, unlocking the power of Niagara. A popular poll in 1909 named four railway presidents among "Canada's Ten Biggest Men," and a journalist noted enthusiastically, "in the knapsack of every Canadian schoolboy there is – not a marshall's baton – but a millionaire's bank book." Another writer could not believe that Donald Mann and William Mackenzie were motivated by self-interest in the creation of their personal transcontinental railway, the Canadian Northern; their actions could only be explained as an act of patriotism.[3]

Others, though, were less than enthusiastic about the achievements and values of men of wealth. Throughout the pre-1914 decades spokesmen for labour and agrarian movements attacked the Canadian plutocrats as oppressors of the industrial worker and the homesteader. Clergy of both Protestant and Catholic denominations stopped automatically identifying wealth with virtue and began to question the assumptions of what seemed to be an age of unrestrained acquisitiveness. Intellectuals ranging from Goldwin Smith through Principal Grant, Henri Bourassa, Andrew Macphail, and Stephen Leacock condemned the way in which "business values" turned everything human into cold yellow metal. In 1914 the American muckraker, Gustavus Myers, published *A History of Canadian Wealth*, arguing that most of the great Canadian fortunes were based on special privilege, subsidies, and corruption. In the same year, in *Arcadian Adventures with the Idle Rich*, Stephen Leacock sketched the new Plutoria (Montreal) peopled by ruthless amoralists and feather-brained pseudo-aristocrats whose lives corroded religion, education, politics, and common morality. Already in 1900, a poet had summarized the intellectuals' response to the advent of that new Canadian phenomenon, the millionaire: he was, wrote Archibald Lampman, "A creature of that old distorted dream/That makes the sound of life an evil cry."[4]

In his 1946 presidential address to the Canadian Historical Association F. H. Underhill said that "liberalism in North America, if it is to mean anything concrete, must mean an attack upon the domination of institutions and ideas by the business man."[5] This statement was typical of the continuing belief held by liberal, "progessive" intellectuals that the values of liberal culture and high profits were necessarily opposed. Businessmen and their activities were entirely comprehensible to anyone who understood the meaning of greed. The history of North American business was the history of the wars of the Robber Barons against the People, worth studying only to know the enemy better. This cast of mind is still common among humanist intellectuals, media personalities, and arts students in universities. Whatever these studies prove, they originated in the belief that neither the past nor the present is quite that simple.

13

Chapter 1

# Success

"In my college days," he said, "I should have considered a plate of oysters an ample meal. I should have asked for nothing more. We eat," he said, "too much."

This, of course, started Mr. Fyshe on his favourite topic. "Luxury!" he exclaimed, "I should think so! It is the curse of the age. The appalling growth of luxury, the piling up of money, the ease with which huge fortunes are made...these are the things that are going to ruin us. Mark my words, the whole thing is bound to end in a tremendous crash. I don't mind telling you, Duke – my friends here, I am sure, know it already – that I am more or less a revolutionary socialist."

> – Stephen Leacock, *Arcadian Adventures with the Idle Rich*

Business was about making money. To many outsiders being in business seemed to be about nothing but making money. Businessmen could be completely and finally understood as the high priests of triumphant materialism. The profit motive was everything in business. The lust for profits explained all business behaviour. The accumulation of profit was the acid test of business success. Surely the house poet of a Vancouver lumber company captured the sum of business aspirations when he wrote,

> You can have your golden sunrise and your sunset rich and
> red,
> You can have your summer rose and autumn peace,
> But give to us the honey time, the honey time instead
> And we'll have every treasure in our reach.

> It's fine to watch the apple when it ripens on the bough,
> It's fine to see the wheat in the bin,
> But there's another season that we're singing for right now,
> We want to see THE MONEY COMING IN.[1]

Other contemporary business comments on money-making, though, struck a very different note. The question of "Our False God" was raised, for example, in a 1910 issue of the *Journal of the Canadian Bankers' Association*. The false god was Mammon and the article was an attack on those who worshipped God in theory and Mammon in practice. The accumulation of great wealth, the writer claimed, tended to spoil a person's moral nature by begetting "self-indulgence or a miserable pride of purse." The poor, on the other hand, were "more charitable and unselfish than the rich and quite as likely to be contented." The article concluded with a protest against the "over-valuation of wealth, however accumulated and however spent, and against the current fashion of calculating success exclusively in dollars."[2] This was not just a token denunciation of sin in one of Satan's house-organs, but was typical of the attacks on Mammon that were the norm whenever businessmen and the business press wrote about money-making and the pursuit of wealth.

Over a thirty-year period there was not one favourable reference to the straightforward goal of making money in Canada's most important business journal, the *Monetary Times*. A representative editorial on the subject in the 1880s quoted extensively from a sermon on the text, "He that is greedy of gain troubleth his own house." In the 1890s "the greatest danger of the time on this continent" was found to be "the idea that money overtops everything else." In 1901 the journal reprinted a warning from *Success* magazine that rich men may awake late in life to find they have destroyed all the finer things in their nature during the cold, sordid search for wealth. "The greed of gold," the budding entrepreneur was warned, "has become a devastating passion, leaving nothing but Dead Sea fruit in the grasp of its unfortunate victim." In 1906 one of the main "troubles of prosperity," the editors found, was "the wild race for success at any price to which it seems to have given rise."[3]

The Canadian *Journal of Commerce* worried about "Modern Extravagance," the burning desire to have riches to spend on luxuries that was pervading North American society in 1891. The *Financial Post* in 1907 was routinely advising young men to reject the attitude that a person had to make money to keep up with the parade. *Le Moniteur du Commerce* had filled its columns for months in 1886 with advice to merchants and clerks not to make the simple accumulation of money the aim of life: "soyez plus qu'une machine à faire de l'argent; soyez un homme." Twenty years later it was chastising Canadians for following "le précepte américain: 'Fais de l'argent honnêtement, si tu peux, mais fais de l'argent.'" The *Canadian Grocer* spread to the trade a presidential address to the Toronto Retail Grocers' Association warning merchants not to be "carried away with that insane idea, that the almighty dollar constitutes everything for which you strive." A noted speech to the Winnipeg Board of Trade on "Going Into Business" concluded with remarks on the utter sadness of the "rich failure," the man who had spent his career "worshipping with ever increasing veneration the golden calf." Joseph Flavelle, president of National Trust and the William Davies pork packing company, wrote Robert Borden that "absorption in material affairs is fatal to idealism." John Northway, a dry goods merchant, noted in his diary with admiration an encounter with two young relatives whose character was "far superior to the having of mere money." In the midst of Canada's Gilded Age there was B. E. Walker, president of the Bank of Commerce and the high priest of Canadian finance, advising Y.M.C.A. men that he could "imagine no failure in life so ghastly as the man who has learned nothing but how to accumulate money," warning members of the Schoolmen's Club that Canada could never be a truly great nation if the measure of our national status was money, prophesying to the Montreal Canadian Club that Canada could not survive if it believed only in "success as represented by money," writing to the *Globe* that "we are at present too much in love with material prosperity," writing to a friend that though he favoured penny banking systems to encourage habits of thrift he did not want them attached to public schools "because I think we have too much commercialism in Canada as it is," and writing privately to a clergyman that "it will be a great pity if in Canada we cannot give our younger people a better aim in life than mere money-making."[4] Even the supposed hymn to money-making previously quoted was set in the modifying context of reminding businessmen that it was the season to begin collecting debts. Nowhere in the representative sources from which these statements have been culled are there naked statements advocating materialism, greed, or concentration on getting wealthy.

Business spokesmen were not entirely foolish, and quite understood the apparent anomaly of being in business but not being interested in making money. They actually directed their arguments against only certain attitudes and practices involved in the pursuit of wealth. There was nothing wrong with accumulating wealth, they believed, so long as one went about it in the right way. The right ways to success had not markedly changed since the days of *Poor Richard's Almanack*. Industry, integrity, and frugality were still the qualities without which success in life was impossible. There was never a hint that any other patterns of behaviour could lead to enduring or satisfying success in business.

The *Monetary Times'* 1910 symposium on success was typical: J. H. Brock of Great West Life condemned the use of tobacco and alcohol, claiming that success was largely a function of good character. Frederic Nicholls, general manager of Canadian General Electric and a director of hosts of enterprises, announced, "any progress I may have made I attribute to a conscientious attempt to live up to the Civic Motto of the City of Toronto, viz. Industry, Intelligence, Integrity." Lumber baron and Senator the Hon. W. C. Edwards echoed Ben Franklin in his proclamation that "the first requisite to success is honesty, the next is good habits and fixity of purpose, the next, industry and perseverance."[5] One of the best summations of the orthodox maxims for success had appeared in the *Canada Lumberman* in 1903:

Things to be Remembered

1. The value of time. Lost capital may be restored by diligent use of experience; time lost is lost for ever.
2. The success of perseverance. "Keeping everlastingly at it" brings the hoped-for result.
3. The pleasure of working. The only really unhappy, rich or poor, are the idle.
4. The dignity of simplicity. When the "frills" are off the man is "on."
5. The worth of character. In the last analysis the only real value is a clear conscience.
   . . .
8. The obligation of duty. Your concern should not be so much what you get, as what you do for what you get.
9. The wisdom of economy. The man who saves makes more than he saves.
10. The virtue of patience. "All things come to him who waits."
    . . .
12. The joy of originating. The happiest man is he who does the best things first. The creative instinct should be encouraged for the pure joy found in its demonstrations. The subsequent financial reward brings no such pleasure as that first sense of having made a new thing or conceived a new idea.[6]

The basic problem the desire to make money posed for anyone aiming at true success was in the way it tempted individuals to violate the code of hard work, honesty, and saving. The "get-rich-quick" mentality could be fatal to any young man who thought the end of making money was more important than the proper means of making it. The maxim "make no haste to be rich if you would prosper"[7] neatly captured the paradox of an ethic that taught present restraint in the hope of future success. One could want to have wealth, but not too badly. Formulations of the principle littered Canadian success literature. One businessman warned the young men of the British American Business College "not to be anxious about early becoming rich, for a determination to be rich early was pretty sure to end in disappointment." W. C. Edwards concluded his remarks on success with the caution that "Nothing [is] more dangerous than a desire to hastily become rich. There are perhaps more men poor from the desire to hastily become rich than from any other cause."[8]

Too much greed could lead a person to ignore any or all of the basic building blocks leading to enduring success. In the extreme, greed could lead to dishonesty, which was never condoned at any level of business. Businessmen had to deal with one another, often in verbal or trust relationships. They at least had to uphold the principle of honesty among thieves. A fairly typical, if extravagant, sermon to young men on honesty was printed in the introductory pages of J. E. Hansford's *The Business Guide*:

> Remember that honesty rises above fortune and above kings; by that alone, and not by the splendor of riches or of titles is glory acquired, that glory which it will be your happiness and pride to transmit unspotted to your posterity. Honesty is greatness itself; dishonesty never made a man great, and never will. Rather be and continue poor, while others around grow rich by fraud and disloyalty, rather be without place or power, while others beg their way upward; rather bear the pain of disappointed hopes, while others win their way by flattery, and forego the gracious pressure of the hand for which others cringe and crawl. Wrap yourself in the cloak of virtue, and seek your bread with an honest hand, and if you grow grey in this cause, with unsoiled honor bless God, and rejoice.

> "The honest man, though e'er so poor,
> Is king of men for all that."[9]

The desire to have things could also be fatal to success if it meant dissipating wealth in personal consumption, in luxurious and extravagant habits of living. Extravagance was the expenditure rather than the investment of capital. No one could hope to accumulate capital without practising thrift, which meant that the man who wanted money had to live without it for the greater part of his life. Accordingly, would-be money-makers had first to realize they must do without the things money could buy. How painful it was to see a merchant "launch out" into theatre-going, club-frequenting, seaside-holidaying, and "dressing his children like French fashion plates," when, if he would only live over his shop, keep his own books, and practise in his business and household the economy that was plainly his duty, he could enjoy a comfortable living.[10] Things had come to a dangerous situation in Toronto in 1905 when young men about town indulged themselves in two-dollar ties, ten-dollar meerschaums, and twenty-dollar fur gauntlets: "The town is just rotten with this kind of thing," lamented the *Monetary Times*. "Cabs; supper at McConkey's or Webb's; two dollar seats at the theatre, little games of cards, and so on; and you bet these things mean borrowing money."[11]

Fears that the whole of Canadian society was given to living beyond its means often inspired blanket condemnations of luxury and extravagance. In 1906 the *Journal of Commerce* took a typically dim view of the benefits almost a decade of economic growth had brought to Canadians:

> Anybody who perambulates on one of the fashionable thoroughfares of any of our large cities of an afternoon and observes the well made dresses, hats and footwear of the young people of both sexes can scarcely help considering what a vast amount of money it takes to pay for it all. One does not see an ill-dressed person among them; a beggar would be an anomaly on our streets, for none in Canada but the idle and lazy need want for bread, and that well-buttered too. Every novelty in extravagance finds people eager to possess. The bicycle of a few years ago – which everybody old enough to ride must have, and did have; the automobile of to-day; the expensive furs, which, for the sake of display, are worn even in hot weather; the fast horses and other things no less rapid, together with other various luxuries which recall to those who read history nowadays the manners of Imperial Rome – all tend to show what an extravagant age we live in.[12]

These remarks were addressed to the middle class. Others widened the net by damning the poor for aping the display and self-indulgence of the rich. Modern civilization, it was noted, still possessed "a barbaric taste . . . for splendour qua splendour . . . the craving of beads."*[13]

The problem of wealth became especially engaging when its impact on succeeding generations was considered. A rich man's son was apt to become habituated to an extravagant and luxurious life style. Worse, he would have received these material benefits without having worked for them. Would it be possible, then, for him to have developed the necessary virtues to succeed in life? "Toute ardeur pour le travail lui est enlevée et il traine sa vie . . . comme un de ces êtres dont l'existence n'est d'aucun avantage pour la société et dont la disparition de la scène serait à peine remarqué."[14] Henry Darling, a self-made Toronto merchant, thought wealthy men might as well retire from business and enjoy spending their money, for there was little chance that their offspring would use an inheritance wisely.[15] "Young men who inherit riches may become useful citizens," speculated the *Canadian Grocer,* "The chances are against them." A lumber dealer wrote privately to a friend, "What I have accumulated may be of more injury to those who receive it than a benefit – a good name is the best legacy to receive."[16]

This argument was taken to its logical conclusion. "One of the greatest helpers in the world, as well as one of the finest disciplinary forces," said the *Financial Post*'s self-help columnist, "is poverty." Erastus Wiman, a poor Canadian boy who made good in big business circles in the United States, speculated that the great American fortunes could not be transmitted because the sons of the wealthy did not have "the advantage of being poor. . . . The stimulus of effort from poverty, the necessity of industry, the advantage of thrift and the achievements possible alone to energy of character are all heritages of the poor young man, better fitting him for the battle of life than a fortune left him by the efforts of others." Another Canadian expatriate, Lord Beaver-

---

* On the other hand, the *Journal of Commerce* had once appreciated the social utility of extravagance. In the depression of the 1890s it had recognized the contra-cyclical utility of spending by the wealthy:

Were the wealthier citizens of Montreal to shut down upon spending their incomes freely, were a craze to spread for small economies, were they to take to heart the outcry against the extravagance of the rich, the effect would be seriously disastrous to the business of the city, and none would suffer so much as the industrial classes into whose pockets there ultimately comes the vast bulk of the money spent by the wealthy, for the value of all that contributes to the personal enjoyment of society is derived from labor. A miser is universally hated, and justly, for he is the enemy of industrial life, of capital, and the activities of businessmen. Were all men to turn misers, commerce would be blighted, and civilization would recede. (May 31, 1895, p. 902)

brook, told young men in his success manual that money was "just as likely to be a curse as a blessing." For this reason the man of wealth would care little for leaving his fortune to his descendants: "He knows that they would be better men for going down stripped into the struggle, with no inheritance but that of brains and character. Wealth without either the wish, the brains, or the power to use it is too often the medium through which men pamper the flesh with good living, and the mind with inanity, until death, operating through the liver, hurries the fortunate youth into an early grave. The inheritance tax should have no terrors for the millionaire."[17]

People inclined to personal extravagance were apt to try to achieve instant wealth through gambling or speculation. These habits were always condemned. Although there could be some confusion about exactly what counted as speculation in business, there was never a good word said about gambling or speculation in the abstract. One aspect of the indictment of gambling centred on the fact that most gamblers lost their money, but the practice was nonetheless habit-forming and could lead to immoral behaviour. Variations on this theme were always used to warn the public, especially the poor public, away from speculation. The other theme, always raised when it was asked how legitimate business differed from gambling, was that the latter represented an attempt to obtain something for nothing, to profit without giving in return:

> ... no useful end is served by the operations of betting men; they add nothing to the common stock of conveniences or services which come from business activities, and that make trading so fruitful to the advantage of the community. If a gambler is successful he has secured the money of another person without having given back one particle of value.... The desire to secure the money of others for nothing is a passion that runs a close parallel to the lust which breeds a criminal....
>
> Now the risks incident to all forms of business, are, with very rare exceptions, inspirers of high and virtuous qualities. The business world knows nothing about taking money for nothing; all trade is based upon the exchange of equivalents in some sense. ... Business risks stimulate industry, prudence, honorable faithfulness to engagements, the acquisition of expert skill, and serve to foster the highest moral qualities .... The one is a vice, a social cancer, a demoralizing habit, a foe to industry and to honor, while the life of business builds up society on the firm foundation of individual probity and is the healthy life blood of the body corporate of a nation.[18]

What did the abhorrence of the attempt to get something for nothing mean in concrete terms? In Manitoba after the crash of 1883 it meant there was strong division, ideologically at least, between "the respectable portion of men in business" and the land speculators who had caused so much damage to the North-West in the first three years of the decade. For the next several years the Winnipeg *Commercial* hammered away at the distinction between men who were developing the area by their plodding industry and the "vultures," "parasites," and "sharks" who fed upon the industry of others, producing nothing, adding nothing to the wealth of the country, but taking profits that others had earned. These were not only the real estate agents, but those landlords who hung on to their real estate, trying to pay their debts by taxing legitimate commerce:

> There are two classes ... whose interests are generally as opposite as landlord and tenant, and these are the landlord and the trading classes. The owner of real estate in any city or town, no matter how public spirited he may be, is necessarily more or less a parasite upon the trading community, especially if his real estate be business property; and in the city of Winnipeg the extortionate rents collected by such persons make the demands of Irish landlords in that respect look like extreme moderation if not benevolence to tenants. ... Merchants and manufacturers in this city are working for landlords just as surely as ever were the down-trodden peasantry of France before the great revolution.[19]

Though extreme, the Winnipeg situation was not unique. The *Canadian Manufacturer* thought much the same of Toronto landlords, finding it hard to justify, for example, the income from the Baldwin leaseholds when the family had never invested its money in any productive enterprises. "They toil not but live in luxurious idleness while others create the values from which they derive their income." For a time the journal was an unacknowledged disciple of Henry George, seeing his proposal to tax nothing but land values as the best way of assuring that "parasitism" would not be allowed to bear fruit. Fifteen years later the *Financial Post*, though dedicated to the interests of the investing class, drew sharp distinctions between useful investments in industrials and those which, by tieing up capital in land, did nothing for the country beyond raising the cost of living. In general, there seemed to be an undercurrent of feeling in the business community that real estate operations were closer to pure speculation than to legitimate business. One street railway executive, none too fastidious in his own operations, wrote

23

a friend about a mutual acquaintance who seemed to have a satisfactory character, despite having "the real estate taint about him."[20]

More directly, suspicion of gambling led to frequent denunciations of the transactions on stock and produce markets. During the 1880s the *Monetary Times* was decidedly opposed to dealing in future contracts in commodities and on margin in anything. One editorial came close to calling for abolition of stock exchanges themselves:

> Gambling in its various forms is illegal. And yet what goes on every day at our Stock Exchanges? There men meet together, in person or by proxy, and stake large sums upon the contingency of stocks rising or falling in price. The *bulls* and the *bears* are organized bodies of men, who play with loaded dice. ... They put their loaded dice against the unloaded dice of the public; the game is not fair; it is even more unfair, and therefore more disreputable, than most other forms of gambling. Stock gambling, backed by large amounts of borrowed capital, is the scandal of the day. If gambling in other forms, even where there is no "bank" with the odds in its favor, where the chances are equal and where skill makes the difference, is put down by the strong arm of the law, is it not then an anomaly that a form of gambling in which the chances are not equal, in which there are loaded dice on one side, should be fostered by respectable financial institutions?

About the same time the *Journal of Commerce* was taking the same position on stock exchange transactions, asking in what way brokers and their operations contributed to the progress of the country. Possibly none could complain if they confined themselves to the legitimate business of the country; "but over and above this they are merely a parcel of speculators, more or less reckless, who hardly have any other means of support, ... and by their manipulations disturb the commerce of the country."[21]

Sniping at market speculation continued through the 1890s, directed primarily at trading in commodity futures and options. The Chicago wheat pit was denounced by George Hague, general manager of the Merchants' Bank, as "only another sort of Monte Carlo." The *Journal of Commerce* urged Americans to outlaw such gambling, as Canadians had, because "the farming interest has a clear right to be protected by the State from an evil that like a deadly cancer is feeding upon the life of the grain trade and damaging agricultural interest like a blight." The *Monetary Times* warned Canadian businessmen (who, "with scarcely an exception, conduct their transactions in an honest and straightforward manner") to resist those who would introduce "the American speculative element" into Canadian commerce. For some years it had been upset at the methods of American finance capitalism, believing that stock-watering and manipulation were a kind of "communistic" appropriation which would create a response in kind from the common people. In the worst of the depression in 1894, George Cox used his presidential address to the Bank of Commerce annual meeting as the occasion to criticize the stock and grain speculating public of Canada for losses they had taken on American markets:

It is a pity the law is powerless to restrain them for their own good, and to protect the business morals of the community. Many a Canadian who, by attention to his legitimate business, was developing habits of thrift and industry, which would make him valuable to the community and useful to himself, has been induced to deal in Chicago, has early in his experience made a little money, and has thus been led to feel that the old methods of moderate profits for daily toil were slow and wearisome, but later on, when his speculations went against him, he has found that he has not only lost his money, but has also impaired or lost his habits of perseverance and industry, . . . [22]

Cox differed from these speculators only in doing most of his stock manipulating in Canada. This example of the pot calling the kettle black demonstrated the near impossibility of distinguishing between "legitimate" and illegitimate speculation. No one wanted to prevent investors from being able to buy a few shares of Bank of Montreal or C.P.R. stock and pay 5 or 10 per cent down with the balance at the end of the year. The real problem centred on the resources and capabilities of investors. No one wanted ignorant widows and clergymen to risk their livelihoods speculating on margin. But to stop this might put an unfair restraint on an intelligent, wealthy businessman like Joseph Flavelle. He did not speculate in stocks, he wrote privately, "I however from time to time take very substantial holdings of securities not yet fully proven – in the purchase of which I exercise my judgment based upon an intelligent study of the situation. In these holdings I sometimes use only my own capital, and again in addition I lean upon my bankers."[23] Moreover, although there was still considerable distrust of market manipulation by bulls and bears, trade journals were beginning to understand how a speculative element could facilitate market movements.

In these circumstances business writers began to content them-selves with cries of moral outrage and general warnings to the young and inexperienced. When the speculative craze of 1902-1903 had collapsed there was general approval in principle of Henri Bourassa's proposals in the House of Commons to end stock spec-ulation, but there was equally general feeling that tinkering with the system would not work. Although the *Monetary Times* still felt speculation was a lower form of gambling than betting on horses, (where at least a man knew what he was apt to lose) it now realized that "little can be done by Parliament to check speculation, which seems to be inherent in human nature. Probably the only remedy lies in a continued campaign of education of young men and others including clergymen and widows, as to its worse than uncertain nature." Much the same attitudes were taken to mining specula-tion. Those in the industry who were interested in "mining as a business" complained loudly and bitterly about the coalition of swindlers, shyster lawyers, and newspapers responsible for perpetu-ating the image of "mining as a gamble." No one quite dared, however, to risk discouraging development by interfering with the free play of capital markets. It was always the case, though, that reputable mining and financial men tried to expose frauds and warned the public to stay clear of the fakers given such prominence in the news and advertising columns of the daily press. The business community was at a loss to deal with its slums of speculation; it did broadcast warnings to the innocent that they entered at their peril.*[24]

Businessmen's understanding of the workings of the natural laws of economics also reinforced the suspicion of speculation. What caused depressions, after all, but an excess of speculative fervour, unsound business practices which rebounded in crashes and fail-ures, liquidation and belt tightening? The *Financial Post's* analysis of the recession of 1907-1908 was typical: "The prosperity of the three years from 1905 to 1907 came too suddenly. We got rich too quickly, with the usual result, that we were extravagant in the expenditure of our newly gotten gains. Hence came the speculation in western lands and eastern stocks, the over-expansion of new industries, the too ready lending of bank funds for new undertak-ings, and a pervasive extravagance in ordinary life. The year 1908 corrected that style of existence and our accounts have been in pro-

* If these attitudes to gambling seem naive beyond belief see the incident recounted in James Frazier Wall, *Andrew Carnegie* (New York, 1970), pp. 799-802, in which Charles M. Schwab felt duty-bound to resign the presi-dency of U.S. Steel in 1901 because of incorrect newspaper reports that he had broken the bank at Monte Carlo.

cess of adjustment. . . . We have learnt the lesson of caution." In this framework depressions became a legitimate form of "punishment" (a favourite term of B. E. Walker's in his comments on the state of the economy) for business sins. To business moralists these setbacks were "only right" because they had the good effect of teaching that "we can only earn our bread by the sweat of our brow." A boom, according to the *Canadian Mining Review*, inevitably meant "business conducted under the influence of temporary insanity, stimulated by more or less knavery." A depression was an almost welcome collective return to those conditions of poverty that in nations as well as individuals gave rise to the sound virtues of industry, integrity, and thrift.[25]

The commitment to the work ethic evident in these strains of business thought hardly needs comment. Work was the source of all value, all worth. It was the law set down for man after the tragedy of Eden, "la grande loi imposée à l'homme sur cette terre . . . pour l'homme le premier des devoirs et la première des nécessités." Hard, patient work – "steady plodding," "laborious training and discipline" – was as opposite to the speculative spirit as night to day. The dominant theme of success advice was always to urge young men to "work, hard work, intelligent work, and then more work." This was one of J. J. Hill's maxims for success. It was echoed by Lord Strathcona, one of the near-mythical titans of the C.P.R., in one of his few recorded comments on success:

Any success I may have had in life is due in a great measure to the somewhat Spartan training I received during my Aberdeen apprenticeship. . . . I had but few wants and no distractions to draw me away from the work I had in hand. It was impressed upon me from my earliest years by one of the best mothers that ever lived that I must aim at being a thorough master of the work by which I had to get my living, and to be that I must concentrate my whole energies on my work, whatever it might be, to the exclusion of every other thing. I soon discovered that if I ever accomplished anything in life it would be by pursuing my object with a persistent determination to attain it. I had neither the training nor the talents to accomplish anything without hard work, and fortunately I knew it.[26]

Businessmen strongly resented critics on the left denying them the status of workers. There was nothing wrong with the labour theory of value – indeed it was a central article of their faith – nor in the idea that wealth rightfully belonged to the labour that produced it. The socialist fallacy was to ignore "brain labour" which was by far the most valuable kind of labour. This was a fundamental axiom of thought about work in the business community, and there was a general consensus that "the theory that mental effort is not labor, is too shallow to merit serious consideration."[27] Businessmen always worked hard, often harder than employees who enjoyed fixed hours and limited responsibility. They did the most difficult work, the organizing, managing, and predicting that caused immense nervous strain. Certainly it was possible to divide people into classes according to their work; but the proper divisions would be between the useful and the useless, the workers and the drones, and this would cut directly across the artificial class lines drawn by the left. Busy men and idle men could be found at every level in the worlds of capital and labour.[28]

What did businessmen work for? Surely profits had to be at the root of it all. Certainly they were, but businessmen emphasized other satisfactions and achievements that stemmed from their activities. Sir Edmund Walker claimed it was a finer thing in his life to have created a great Canadian institution (the Bank of Commerce) than to have made millions. Many years earlier a pioneer sewing-machine manufacturer had told a banquet that "he felt as though he could throw his whole soul into the business, and when he saw 200 or 300 tons of pig iron in his yard, he always thought of how that dull mass of iron could be moulded into life. ... This was their business, and it was a grand and noble work, doing away with much arduous labor that was formerly necessary." Comparing himself to those businessmen who viewed a company only as a hewer and drawer in the cause of high dividends, Joseph Flavelle instanced Adam Bede's love of craftsmanship for its own sake and urged that the interests of particular shareholders be subordinate to "our positive satisfaction in doing business well for the sake of business." For him, profits would follow naturally as the by-product of effective business service.[29]

When they had to justify their profits businessmen regularly pointed to the services they did provide. A lumberman claimed that nothing contributed so greatly to the prosperity and happiness of a people than the wood he produced – "wood forms the very cornerstone [sic] of modern industrial life." F. H. Clergue, the American entrepreneur who enjoyed a meteoric career as the industrial benefactor of Northern Ontario, told the Toronto Board of Trade in 1900 "how it is possible to go into Algoma, take the raw resources which God left there when the world was created, and turn them to the beneficial use of mankind." Insurance men were prone to the most inflated claims about the way in which their spreading of "the gospel of life insurance" protected wives and children, robbed sorrow of its poignancy, and extracted the sting from death. But whether it was George Cox arguing in the Senate that the nine million-dollar profit on William Mackenzie's development of the Toronto Street Railway was justified in view of the growth of Toronto it had stimulated, Sir William Van Horne instancing the "comfortable homes and good food and good clothes to thousands and millions" that the activities of wealthy men had brought about, or the *Monetary Times* pointing out that the normally human materialism of the entrepreneurs who built the Canadian Northern railway had also opened up new country "in which men may transform their poverty into affluence," businessmen generally found no difficulty justifying their profits as a reasonable reward for the goods and services they created. It was only the stock speculators and occasionally the real estate men who were parasites on the community and got something for nothing.[30]

But one trouble with the success that Canadian enterprise enjoyed in providing a high level of goods and services to the community was the disillusionment that affluence could bring to those who believed in the austerities of the classic success ethic. As an elder statesman in the 1920s, Sir Clifford Sifton found himself, according to J. W. Dafoe,

> ... somewhat in the position of the old Roman lamenting the decadence of the commonwealth. The jazz age, in its tempo and its spirit, was centuries away from the days of his youth – a period when clean living, hard work, the treasuring of high ambitions with the fitting of one's self to the efficient achievement of these ambitions, were the approved virtues of the young. The unquenchable appetite for pleasures and thrills; the impatience of authority; the repugnance to hard work; the indifference to the experience of age; the contempt for the old standards of habits and duties – these ... filled him with deep concern for the rising generation, and for the country's future.

Receiving an honourary degree from Queen's in 1927, Sifton told the graduates how he had worked fourteen to sixteen hours a day for most of his active life. They were the happiest days of his life and his rewards were exactly proportionate to the work he had done. It was a result of the "strenuous" life he had been taught to lead in his youth:

> Forty years ago the gospel of thrift and methodical energy were taught. Boys heard nothing else than that if they wanted to get on in the world they had to work, and work hard: that their future depended entirely upon themselves. Even their

29

[*sic*] horrible examples of idle rich men's sons were not wanting. We all understood it. Most of us acted upon it. I should think it would be a good idea to start this propaganda again. The gospel of idleness – less work, more amusements which in one way or the other are paid for by the public, is the old doctrine again which ruined ancient Rome – *panem et circenses* – free bread and the circus.[31]

Joseph Flavelle was also deeply concerned in the 1920s by the way the spirit of service had been replaced by individual selfishness. The great increase in spending power in wartime, he thought, had led to a public obsession with "what we are pleased to call a standard of living, which in plain terms was a standard of extravagance." The churches had emptied as the wealthy trooped off to golf courses or went motoring on weekends, with even "tens of thousands of workpeople and their families spending the Sunday picnicing, or out of doors in their Ford or other cheap cars." Because people had wealth and wanted more there was no longer a commitment to notions of duty, discipline, and individual effort; only a restless collective clamour that "rights" be respected. How could a people spoiled by affluence recapture the qualities that led to true progress; for "the story of life's accomplishment is the story of improvement forced upon men through struggle?"[32]

In the depths of the Great Depression men of affairs schooled in the old virtues would still think in these categories. The response of the millionaire Prime Minister, R. B. Bennett, to the Depression was very much within this tradition. He consciously recalled the 1880s when people had worked their way out of their difficulties rather than relying on the government to take care of them. "The fibre of some of our people has grown softer and they are not willing to turn in and save themselves. They now complain because they have no money. When they were earning money many of them spent it in speculation and luxury. 'Luxury' means anything a man has not an immediate need for, having regard to his financial position." Bennett hoped the Depression would induce men and women "to think in terms of honest toil." If it did not, "the end of organised society is not far distant." In 1933 he told an assembly of students in Toronto, "one of the greatest assets that any man or woman can have entering life's struggle is poverty."[33]

So the values proclaimed by men in business were radically different from the "business values" critics were beginning to attack before World War I. Business spokesmen approved of Henri Bourassa's attack on speculation. They echoed his and others' warnings about the cult of the "veau d'or." They, too,

**A HUNDRED YEARS LATER**
SHADE OF WESLEY–"And this is Methodism!
I should hardly have known it!"

worried about the debilitating effects the desire to get rich quickly had on character and the danger that the extravagance of the poor would keep them in poverty. "The greed of gain" and "the vulgar ostentation of the common rich"[34] were no more valued within business than outside it. When Stephen Leacock ridiculed the conspicuous consumption and leisure of the elite of Plutoria, when he portrayed "Wizards of Finance" who had been created by good luck and haphazard gambling, when he described how wealth corrupted the offspring of wizards of finance, he was saying little more about modern Canadian business than were the Walkers, the Flavelles, or the editors of the *Monetary Times* and the *Journal of Commerce*. They were all worrying about a society in which the bases of economic success – hard work and plain living – were in constant danger of being undercut by the desire for rapid success and the immediate enjoyment of success.

How much of this stew of platitudes, pious incantations, and common sense did anyone in business take seriously? Did anyone believe in the gospel of success? Did businessmen practise it? Were all the speeches, self-help columns, and righteous editorializing no more than ceremonial posturing, usually for the benefit of employees? Tentative answers to these questions are attempted in the Conclusion. In the meantime it is suggestive to consider one of the central axioms of all discussions of success: that real success was not necessarily the achievement of wealth. No one who preached the success gospel ever promised that it would inevitably pay off materially. Cultivation of the right qualities was apt to bring a modest competence, but there had never been enough high positions in industry and great rewards to shower upon everyone who strove for them. Those who had them – who were superficially successful – might not have obtained them by legitimate means. In its ultimate implications the success ethic had little or nothing to do with making money, everything to do with the cultivation of moral character.

But the real world of business had a lot to do with making money. Businessmen who worked hard, dealt honestly, and lived frugally, but still did not make money, were business failures. What did a businessman do when by his own light he had played the self-help game to the limit but was not making money at it? How far could the ordinary businessman trust Benjamin Franklin and Poor Richard?

Chapter 2

# The Flight from Competition

Men go into business to earn a living. There are often circumstances which seriously interfere with their ability to do so. The greatest of these is competition.

– *Canadian Grocer*, 1891

In the autumn of 1883 the wholesale grocers of Hamilton and Toronto met to discuss the possibility of doing something about ruinous price-cutting in the articles they sold. By early 1884 Montreal grocers had formed an association to deal with the same problem and in June the two groups came together to form the Dominion Wholesale Grocers' Guild, branches of which were soon established in other Ontario and Quebec wholesale centres. The Guild's first actions were to regulate terms of credit and discounts, but it soon began arranging price-fixing agreements with manufacturers of tobacco, starch, baking powder, pickles, and other products. In each case the Guild fixed the prices under which the manufacturer's goods were to be resold to retailers and the manufacturer enforced the terms by refusing to sell to any price-cutting wholesaler except at higher prices. The most significant of these agreements was reached with the sugar refineries in the summer of 1887; sales of white sugar would be made to Guild members on more favourable terms than to non-members, membership in the Guild being conditional on accepting its fixed prices and doing no retailing. The Guild promised the refiners that members' profit margin on sales of sugar to retailers would not exceed one-half cent per pound. Sugar accounted for about 40 per cent of the grocery trade in the late 1880s and had been the article in which price-cutting had been universal.[1]

Outrage at the price-fixing arrangements entered into by the wholesale grocers was a major cause of Canada's first investigation of combinations in restraint of trade, carried out by a Select Committee of the House of Commons in the spring of 1888. Neither the investigation nor the ensuing anti-combines legislation of 1889 had the slightest effect on the Wholesale Grocers' Guild's price-fixing arrangements. Old agreements stayed in effect; new agreements on woodenware, rice, starch, and molasses were reached in 1890 and 1891. Discipline of price-cutting wholesalers was tightened. The only change in the Guild's method was that the press was no longer supplied with the details of decisions, although the trade press still had inside information.[2]

Continual battles with renegade wholesalers and frustrated retailers led to the collapse of the sugar agreement in 1892. The combines in other articles soon dissolved and the Guild was largely moribund in the mid-1890s, the period that not coincidently saw a major weeding out of wholesale grocers. Beginning in 1898 there was a gradual reorganization and reconstruction of the agreements and the Guild began to function effectively once again. Its methods became standardized into an insistence that manufacturers practise resale price maintenance (legal in Canada) under the covert threat of a boycott (illegal after 1900) by the Guild members. A typical threat was delivered to a manufacturer by the Guild secretary in 1908:

> As you are aware conditions of trade are such that the only authority which can fix prices is the manufacturer and in his own interest and that of the trade it is clearly advisable that the manufacturer protect all wholesalers handling his goods, as otherwise, should a fair profit not be assured, the wholesale trade will cease to take an interest in the sale of his goods and will instead endeavour to push the sale of those goods on which he [sic] can with certainty count on a fair profit.[3]

In these situations the Guild's Price Committee informed the manufacturers what a fair resale price would be. Proceedings were now wholly secret. In 1906 a prosecution for conspiracy was brought against the Guild under the combines section of the Criminal Code. Four years later it was acquitted and went on into World War I stabilizing the trade in its usual way.[4]

The Dominion Wholesale Grocers' Guild was one of the most visible and persistent business organizations in the forefront of a massive flight from domestic competition in the 1880s and 1890s, hard on the heels of the barriers to foreign competition erected by the National Policy tariff. Businessmen formed guilds, associations, pools, trusts, and mergers with the aim of restricting the free market in every form of enterprise – transportation, manufacturing, finance, and distribution. They used a wide variety of methods to attain this end, including written agreements, sworn oaths, bonds, fines, expulsions, boycotts, legally enforced contracts, dumping on foreign markets, "friendly" persuasion, mobilizing public opinion, and bringing in the power of the state. They denied the maxim that competition was the life of trade, and justified their combinations as being in the public interest and in the reasonable interest of honest businessmen who only desired to obtain a "living profit."

Agreements among Canada's great railway systems to fix rates and limit other competitive practices dated from at least 1855 when the Grand Trunk and Great Western agreed to avoid competition. For the next generation agreement after agreement broke down only to be renegotiated and break down again. The amalgamation of the two lines fixed rates permanently in 1883. By then the Grand Trunk was faced with much more serious competition from the Canadian Pacific. Despite their well-publicized antagonism, the management of the two roads turned instinctively to the idea of limiting their competition. The Stephen-Tyler agreement of 1883 "to avoid competition and work together in all respects for mutual benefit" was never implemented, but a working agreement on rates was reached between the general managers in 1884. Other expensive competitive practices, such as running dining cars between Montreal and Toronto, were also eliminated by mutual consent.[5] Formal pacts tended to break down quickly, negotiations were always characterized by mutual distrust and charges of bad faith, and quiet arrangements were sometimes hindered by such public indiscretions as Sir Henry Tyler's remark to the Grand Trunk shareholders just before the 1891 agreement came into effect: "We will now get all we can out of the people of Canada." Nevertheless, efforts to limit competition in transportation continued, for both companies could not help but realize that what Van Horne called "reform in traffic matters" could lead to a saving that "may soon be counted in millions."[6] The Canadian trunk lines were also regular participants in the pools and other associations established by the major American railway systems to regularize rates.

The manufacturers most concerned about competition in the 1880s were the cotton magnates who found their industry in a crisis of surplus capacity by 1883 because of the rush of new capital into the industry after the 1879 doubling of the tariff. A well-publicized "Cotton Congress" in 1883 arranged a scheme of combination that broke down immediately, as did several other attempts to formulate "a price which allows a living profit to the manufacturer." The Canadian Cotton Manufacturers' Association was formed in 1886 to control production, fix minimum prices, and organize dumping of surplus stocks in China. It operated successfully for two years before its collapse from rivalry among New Brunswick manufacturers. The two chief cotton barons of Montreal, David Morrice and A. F. Gault, then organized negotiations resulting in the mass amalgamation of the Canadian mills into the Dominion Cotton Mills Company Limited (1890) and Canadian Coloured Cottons Limited (1892). Controlling approximately 70 per cent of Canadian capacity, these two companies led a general stabilization of cotton production and prices until new mills constructed in the early 1900s necessitated a further merger in 1905, creating the Dominion Textile Company. That merger reduced competition in the industry so much that, with the added help of the tariff on cottons, the shareholders who invested $500,000 in Dominion Textile common stock in 1905 received for the next generation an average annual return of 98 per cent on their capital.[8]

Salt combines had existed off and on in Canada since at least 1871. On March 1, 1889, when anti-combines legislation was before the House of Commons, a new salt syndicate came into effect to purchase the products of all the salt wells in the Dominion, raising the price to consumers from 55 cents to $1.05 per barrel in one day.[9] The Canadian Packers' Association also reorganized in 1889 under the guiding hand of trade paper editor J. B. Maclean, and arranged a very satisfactory limitation of the fruit and vegetable "pack" for that year as well as steady sales at fixed prices.[10] The Canadian Iron Founders' Association had been in existence since 1865, fixing a uniform price for stove and other foundry wares and apparently maintaining regular prices through the whole period. Other manufacturers who had formed associations to fix prices or control entry in the 1880s included biscuit and confectionary makers, cordage and barbed-wire manufacturers, oatmeal millers, and manufacturers of undertakers' supplies.[11]

In 1891 the Canadian Bankers' Association was formed in response to desires that banks exert more political influence and pull together to limit competition. Though the C.B.A. claimed to emphasize bankers' education and professional improvement as its primary goal, it was rightly interpreted in the business press as part of the general movement to restrict competition. There was a successful nation-wide attempt in the early years to fix the maximum rate of interest on savings deposits, and local agreements were reached regarding the handling of certain forms, bills, and special deposits. Rate-fixing agreements seem to have broken down with the founding of new chartered banks in the early years of the twentieth century, but at the time of its incorporation in 1900 the C.B.A. was authorized to supervise the note issues of all chartered banks, manage the system of clearing-houses, and supervise the affairs of any bank that suspended payment.[12]

The most frantic and varied attempts to limit competition were in the areas of wholesaling and retailing, both characterized by too many small businesses struggling for shares of a limited trade. At the local level a simple custom like the giving of Christmas presents could pose a great problem for the ordinary merchant. Grocers, for example, were expected to curry favour with substantial Christmas presents of wine and spirits to customers who played one shop off against another. The only way to end the annual levy was for local grocers to make agreements among themselves – signed pledges not to give any Christmas presents. The anti-Christmas present movement organized by the editors of *Le Prix Courant* in 1889 was estimated to have saved Montreal grocers $12,000. Other centres followed suit.[13] Similarly, early-closing movements were a regular feature of municipal business life in the 1880s and 1890s as merchants struggled to end the competitive scramble of each staying open until there was no more business to do. The first early-closing movements consisted of draft agreements circulated among local merchants for their signature, each pledging to restrict his hours as long as everyone else did. The regular break-down of voluntary agreements led businessmen to ask for government intervention in the form of early-closing by-laws which would restrict hours of business at the request of a certain percentage of merchants in a given trade. Several provinces passed enabling statutes to this effect in the late 1880s and mid-1890s. They were put into effect only with difficulty, for dissenting merchants – usually small retailers struggling to neutralize the advantages of large stores – were able to make much of this legislative interference with the freedom of trade.[14]

Price-fixing agreements to stop the disastrous results of "cutting" were a commonplace of local merchants' associations. In most areas there would be no need for a formal agreement; where there was, a central organization would circulate a standard price list. The Retail Jewellers' Association of Canada, for example, was formed in 1886 and by 1890 had compiled a "living profit price list" which was accepted all over the country and was still in effect for watch repairs in 1900.[15] Local merchants' associations also struggled to limit the number of bankrupt sales at which the stocks of insolvents were sold at cut prices, tried to pressure wholesalers to stop extending credit to incompetents or price-cutters setting up in business to compete with established customers, compiled lists of "deadbeats," and organized restrictions on credit.

The central theme of small business restrictionism was the attempt to maintain lines of demarcation between levels of trade and lines of trade. Wholesalers who sold directly to the public were warned to mind their own business and boycotted by retailers if they did not. At the other extreme, established merchants tried to close off their markets against the "guerilla trade" of salesmen with no stake in their communities – farmers, pedlars, and other transient traders. The pedlar problem, for example, was brought under control by the manipulation of local licensing, although in the city of Toronto not before the Hawkers' and Pedlars' Association had successfully fought a restrictive by-law all the way to the Privy Council.[16] Still more perplexing was the problem of preserving horizontal lines of demarcation between retailers in different lines of trade. "Single-line" merchants found it profitable to carry other lines of goods for the convenience of their customers, as loss-leaders, or as new sources of profitable trade. Druggists tried to carry everything in the way of toiletries, household products, and fancy goods; jewellers stocked hardware; everyone stocked jewellery; grocers sold dry goods and dry goods men sold groceries. The ultimate implications of this kaleidoscopic retailing were brought home to single-line retailers in the 1890s when the founders of Canada's first big department stores moved into one line of goods after another, proclaiming their intention of selling everything. The pioneer department store men, notably Timothy Eaton and Robert Simpson in Toronto, operated on low margins, heavy advertising, and the use of loss-leaders. They also broke with precedent by eliminating credit and by-passing wholesalers in their purchasing. In the early 1890s the department stores wrought havoc with small retailers in Toronto and Montreal; by the end of the decade their mail order business was affecting retailers throughout the Dominion.

Merchants threatened by the department stores fought back with price-fixing schemes, boycotts, and attempts to obtain restrictive legislation. After 1897 the attack on open competition in retailing was led by the Retail Merchants' Association of Canada, whose first action was to sponsor a successful suit against the T. Eaton Company for fraudulent advertising. The R.M.A.C. lobbied for discriminatory taxes on department stores (say, assessing a separate tax on each department in a store), tighter controls on transient traders, and the general institution of resale price maintenance. As its final solution to the problem of stabilizing trade and nullifying the effect of the department stores, the Association proposed "that it would be greatly in the interests of all the laboring, manufactur-ing, commercial and purchasing classes of the Dominion to have all lines of goods belonging to each trade defined in groups by the mutual consent of the Merchants, and a record of them placed upon the Statute books of the Province, and that power be asked to regulate and control by license or otherwise all such groups or lines of trade in cities having a population of 30,000 or more."[17] The R.M.A.C.'s most successful campaign in the early 1900s was the achievement of both provincial and Dominion legislation to pro-hibit the use of trading stamps. These had been introduced in the late 1890s, had become very popular among small merchants, and were quickly seen to be profitable only for the trading stamp com-panies. It was a classic instance of state intervention being the only means of ending a competitive situation from which none of the competitors was benefitting.[18] By 1910 the R.M.A.C. was leading resistance to the incorporation of consumer co-operative societies, posing as the champion of "individualism" in business.

After about 1900 economic expansion and/or fear of the law* may have reduced the incidence of formal agreements in restraint of trade. At the least members of trade associations were now much more careful about the legal implications of their constitutions and by-laws, had little to say to the press, and had mastered techniques of evasion before investigating bodies. When Ontario lumbermen held a special meeting to discuss their situation in 1908, for exam-ple, it was evident that a recent prosecution of Western lumber dealers significantly moderated their desire to reach a formal agree-ment on prices. Telling the press that they were meeting to talk about how to have better times, they did pledge to reduce their cut by 25 per cent; as for prices, the best each man could do was follow one member's advice to "keep your pecker up."[19]

Other businessmen had turned to organic mergers rather than

---

* The combines investigation of 1888 had led to the passing of an utterly useless anti-combines act in 1889, which had been incorporated into the Criminal Code in 1892. In 1900 the law was accidently given baby teeth when an amendment to the relevant section of the Criminal Code omitted the crucial invalidating word. This happened without anyone, including its initiator, real-izing the significance of the change until 1903 when the first of several actions was launched against price-fixing trade associations. The handful of prosecu-tions in the next few years heightened public awareness of and opposition to combines, as did the continuing anti-trust agitation in the United States, and eventually forced the Federal Government to a further attempt to clarify the legislation in the Combines Investigation Act of 1910. This, too, was a largely ceremonial attack on combinations and did not represent a serious legislative attempt to restore open competition in business. For further detail see my article, "Another Anti-Trust Tradition: Canadian Anti-Combines Policy, 1889-1910," *Business History Review* 47, No. 2 (Summer, 1973), pp. 177-88.

loosely knit trade associations as a way of ending open competition. Although the classic merger movement of 1909-1912, in which some 275 individual firms were reduced to 58, was largely defended in terms of the desirability of achieving economies of scale in production and distribution, the need to eliminate "wasteful" competition was obviously a factor in some of the outstanding mergers.[20] And whether legal or not, trade associations continued their restrictive practices. "Notwithstanding ... the Statute books," commented the *Retail Merchants' Journal* in 1907, "it is well known to most businessmen in Canada that agreements are now made and entered into in many lines of trade, with a view of preventing ruinous and unfair competition ... and to act as a pendulum to regulate and steady trade."[21]

This brief description of restrictive activities has concentrated on only the most successful, the most persistent, or the most publicized of the combines and associations formed in the period. An exhaustive list of the combinations mentioned in trade journals or claimed to exist by newspapers would extend into every nook and cranny of the Canadian business world. When hardware men convened in Toronto in 1894, for example, meetings were held of the Wire Nail Association, the Wire Association, the Screw Association, the Bolt and Nut Association, the Rivet Association, the Barb Wire Association, the Bar Iron Association, the Cut Nail Association, the Horseshoe Association, the Tack Association, and the Paint Grinders' Association. All discussed prices. As early as 1887 the *Journal of Commerce* remarked, "there are few branches of trade in this or any other country which are not represented by associations which seek to prevent unprofitable competition." In 1890 N. Clarke Wallace, who had been chairman of the 1888 Select Committee, complained about attempts to burden the people with combines "from the cradle to the grave ... – from Nestle's food in infancy to the coffin in which they were carried to the grave."[22]

A number of businessmen and business organizations actively resisted the tendency to limit free competition. The consolidation of the railroad systems in central Canada in the early 1880s, for example, produced an outburst of anti-monopoly sentiment among shippers frightened at the freedom the Grand Trunk and C.P.R. now had to raise rates without check. Writing in the *Trader* on behalf of small shippers, W. K. McNaught, a Toronto jeweller, rang the changes on railway monopoly as skillfully as any Granger:

From present appearances it seems doubtful whether in the near future the railways won't control this country, instead of the country controlling the railways. . . . Corporations are said to be soulless, and these are not exceptions to the rule, as any one may judge from the past record, either of the Grand Trunk or the Canadian Pacific. They have each bled the public. . . .

We have often pointed out the fact that these railroads are like huge vampires, slowly sucking the life-blood of this country's commerce. They charge the extreme limit the law allows, and in many cases go beyond it, and the sufferers from their legalized tyranny have no chance of redress.

The *Canadian Manufacturer* chimed in with mutterings about "the oppressive and depressing feeling, in the public breast, of utter helplessness, and of being in forced submission to the despotism of a railway monopoly." In the same years in Manitoba the Winnipeg *Commercial* made common cause with farmers in attacking the monopoly rights of the C.P.R., "a horse-leech, which sucks at the life of the country and in its voracity is ever shouting for more." Pressure from urban Boards of Trade led to the establishment of the Royal Commission on Railways in 1886 at which many Manitoba and Ontario shippers called for a railway commission to regulate the systems; when the Canadian Board of Railway Commissioners was finally established in 1902 the Canadian Manufacturers' Association proudly took credit for leading the movement on behalf of government intervention.[23]

All the time it had been trying to shackle railways with government regulation, the C.M.A.'s main aim had been to encourage limiting the competition of foreign manufacturers in the Canadian market. The *Commercial* was the Winnipeg Board of Trade's mouthpiece in the anti-monopoly agitation; but representing other sections of its constituency it also led the campaign for price-fixing in Manitoba retail circles. W. K. McNaught, advocate of railway competition, was an enthusiastic supporter and member of the wholesale jewellers' combine, which at one time offered a $300 reward to anyone bringing evidence of price-cutting by any member. He believed that "combination for protection was a perfectly praiseworthy and legitimate thing to do" and the "very foundation stone" of their association was "honor."[24] Like many other Ontario manufacturers of this period he would go on to play a prominent role in the fight against private power monopolies in the province. At exactly the same time he was lobbying for federal legislation to restrict competition in the jewellery trade.[25]

The same pattern of tarnished virtue was revealed in the struggles against the Wholesale Grocers' Guild. George Light-

41

bound, a Montreal wholesale grocer, was the key witness against the Guild and its sugar combine at the investigation of 1888. He objected to anyone trying to tell him how to run his own business, claimed a perfect right to buy or sell at whatever price he chose, and suggested that businessmen who could not conduct their affairs without a combination should choose another line of business. Under close questioning, however, it was revealed that Lightbound had been one of the charter members of the organization, had taken the lead in originating the combines on tobacco, baking powder, and starch, and had been the first to suggest it was time to fix a combined price on sugar. The trouble with the sugar agreement had arisen only because Lightbound would not join it for the territory west of Montreal, though he was perfectly willing to combine on prices for the south and east. Lightbound was in fact back in the Guild at the time of testifying against it. He claimed he had been squeezed back in only to be able to purchase sugar; actually his firm continued to participate in the sugar combine until November 1893 when it withdrew from all price-fixing because of what it called the "foolish policy" adopted by some members in "demoralizing" the fruit business.[26]

Other witnesses at the 1888 inquiry were caught in similar contradictions. In certain competitive situations they had broken with combines. In other real or posited competitive situations they would go along with combines in the interests of "fair" profits or "legitimate" trade. Walter Paul, a Montreal retailer who testified against the Guild, was "strongly in favour of freedom of business, the survival of the fittest," and yet he had recently been a member of a deputation of retailers insisting that wholesalers not sell directly to the public.[27] In 1890 retail grocers across Ontario and Quebec turned against the Guild, damning it as "the most selfish and unjust organization on the face of the earth today," and calling on its members to "act like business men, not afraid of one another, no matter how low the cut." At exactly the same time these local retailers' associations were continuing their price-fixing – entering new arrangements regarding bread in Toronto and liquor in Montreal – and their attacks on the Guild ended immediately when it agreed to revise credit terms and give larger volume discounts.[28]

Only a small handful of businessmen adopted a consistent, principled resistance to combinations in restraint of trade. A crusty old Montreal wholesale grocer, J. A. Mathewson, had refused to join the Wholesale Grocers' Guild from the beginning, testified against its "malicious blackmail" and "slavery" at every opportunity, and alone among the businessmen opposed to combines in 1888 continued to fight for strong laws against "these infamous, unlawful organizations." The T. Eaton Company was adept at identifying itself as the consumer's friend and made backhanded slaps in its catalogues at merchants who worked merely for profit and wanted to divide the trade so everyone could ride in carriages. Eaton's aimed to do the best it could by each customer, sold good products at the lowest possible prices, and, "we mind our own business." Joseph Flavelle of the Davies meat-packing company took great pride in never having participated in a price-fixing agreement and complained bitterly to Mackenzie King in 1910 that the Combines Investigation bill pending before Parliament would subject honourable firms like his to unfair harassment. The more common objection to that Act was uttered by Senator W. C. Edwards, president of the Canada Cement Company (a firm resulting from a merger that had been directly aimed at achieving monopoly) who thought the Act would deny people "the profit of their industry." He delivered this speech the same week he told the *Monetary Times* that Ben Franklin had written all a young man needed to know about success.[29]

Sporadic complaints by businessmen subjected to the prices charged by combinations and monopolies and the objections to combinations by a few principled free traders were almost totally submerged in a climate of business opinion that attacked open competition as being destructive of profits, security, and business morality. Although lip service was often paid to the notion of competition as the life of trade, the arguments of trade restrictionists subverted the maxim by noting that unfair or illegitimate competition was the death of trade and then defining these unacceptable forms of competition so widely that they stretched almost all the way around the concept.

The "unfair" competitor was thought to be someone who had a privilege not available to his rivals. But what did this mean? Most small-town merchants thought it was unfair for pedlars to be permitted to compete with them without having to pay local taxes. Wholesalers selling at retail or even large retailers who could obtain volume discounts seemed to be operating from a basis of special power if not special privilege. When they took advantage of their position to launch price wars by cutting prices below cost or using loss-leaders, they were treating their competitors particularly unfairly. Indeed, any kind of underselling based on a superior capital position seemed unfair. The merchant who laid aside certain portions of his capital as a kind of "war reserve," argued a writer, "and spends it in price cutting just as an honest man may spend it in advertising or wages, is guilty of an act which it is hard to distinguish from the course of the man who hires some one to burn down the factories and warehouses of troublesome competitors."[30]

It was a small step from the idea of unfair competition to the belief that any competition involving price-cutting was illegitimate. Doing business on "sound business principles" seemed obviously to mean selling goods at a profit. Therefore, according to the *Canadian Grocer,* "selling below cost . . . is commercial idiocy." It hurt oneself, one's creditors, and, as another journal claimed, meant "doing an injustice to the general mercantile community – whose honest aim it ought to be to make a profit." There was no way that merchants in a community could avoid adopting the methods of ignorant or unscrupulous competitors, for the cut prices of one businessman set the levels of the market. A single reckless trader operating on borrowed capital could destroy the profitability of the trade of a whole community while he pursued his stupid course to bankruptcy. A typical outbreak of this "promiscuous" price-cutting in an "out of the way place" like Edmonton in 1887 led the Winnipeg *Commercial* to sermonize on the general issue:

Cutting prices is an offence the most senseless and at the same time the least excusable which any business man can engage in. It is an offence against legitimate trade of a most grave nature, and which should not be condoned in any quarter. No rules or principles in commercial economy can be deduced to prove that any permanent advantage can come from cutting prices below a fair or living profit. . . .

The only legitimate way to do business is to obtain a fair, living profit upon all commodities . . . the opposite system of cutting prices is demoralizing and destructive to legitimate trade, under whatever circumstances indulged in.[31]

The "demoralization" of trade as a result of price-cutting was a favourite business term. It had the obvious implications of a collapse in the regular price structure, leading to furious price juggling. But it also connoted the literal de-*moral*-izing effect of extreme competition in forcing businessmen back into unethical practices they would rather avoid. A retail grocer wrote to the *Canadian Grocer* in 1889 complaining that the only way he could make a profit under prevailing conditions was to deceive his customers by selling six plugs as a "pound" of tobacco when it actually took seven to make that weight. How could a retail man "hold up the dignity of his manhood," "do right," and still stay in business, he asked. "It seems almost impossible for a man behind the counter to be truthful, honourable, straightforward and honest, and succeed." In a similar vein the *Journal of Commerce* argued that when cotton was sold at "cut-throat" prices the only way manufacturers could show "a living profit" was by "the employment of all those tricks of adulteration which have gained some European mills such an unenviable notoriety." Regulation of competition, then, was necessary to preserve the ethical as well as the material bases of business success.[32]

A further connotation of "demoralizing" trade was the effect it had on competitors' morale. Ruthless competition forced the businessman to be on his guard at all times, never secure from day to day. One fierce battle could ruin a life's work. A retail grocer described a situation in his town where four different travellers had appeared in succession quoting four different prices on sugar. By luck he had made a profit in his sugar transaction, but it was pure luck. The local trade "felt sick" at this kind of situation, and all favoured the Guild's one-price system under which "there is not that feeling that every one is buying goods cheaper than you." Commenting on the Guild, Professor W. J. Ashley of the University of Toronto also worried that worship of the consumer led people to forget "the worry and laceration of the spirit" (as well as "the vulgarization of business") involved in perpetual competition. The longing among businessmen for security, financial and otherwise, prompted the *Monetary Times* to suggest that the guild system of early times, though it occasionally seemed "to bear hard upon individual liberty," alleviated many of the scandals of modern trade: "The pushing and 'cutting' and striving for business which characterizes modern methods were then almost unknown.... The life of a trader in those days was one of comparative comfort and ease. Yet the wants of the community were as well supplied as they are now. This is the essential matter, after all."[33]

Members of combines always asked what was unreasonable about joining together to ensure one another "a living profit." Many of them claimed that the alternative to combines was to go out of business and pointed out that "the consumer must not expect the trade of the Dominion to work for them [*sic*] for nothing." This implied that profits in business were nothing more than the wages of businessmen. The Retail Merchants' Association called for "fair wages – improperly called by some, profits"; and a Quebec pharmacist thought it was necessary to interfere with the "incontestablement bon . . . *principe*" of free trade because "dans tout corps social bien organisé, ceux qui exercent les divers états ou métiers qui le composent ont droit à une protection efficace qui leur assure un part des revenus proportionée à leurs aptitudes, à leur application au genre et au montant d'affaires qu'ils transigent." This strain of thought was based on the idea of there being a reward "justly" due to the man who provided a service to the community.[34]

Some people could and did say that open competition was justified as leading to "the survival of the fittest." This was heatedly denied. "To say that a half-witted man, who has money enough to outstay a poorer but able rival, shows himself thereby to be a fitter man than his rival is nonsense," argued the *Canadian Grocer* in an article attacking this usage of "the cant of the evolution theory." Generally, when businessmen used the catch phrases of Social Darwinism, they used them to describe the competitive situation as it existed, not as they hoped it might be. "If this competition continues, it is simply a question of the survival of the fittest," complained a cotton man trying to organize a merger. Another writer agreed that modern society did encourage the survival of the fittest. He meant that only the strongest of the strong could survive. Self-preservation therefore required combination. "What better argument could we have for the existence of the Canadian Bankers' Association?"[35]

The enthusiasts of combination always argued that restraints on competition either actively benefitted or at least did not harm the public. Almost everyone admitted there were limits beyond which trade restraints should not be pressed. It was common to distinguish between good and evil combines, responsible and extortionate ones, just as the distinction was drawn between fair and unfair competition. Just as they could find very little competition that was fair, however, restrictionists seldom found any unfair or extortionate combines operating in Canada, except possibly the railways. The only really evil ones were almost always American: Standard Oil, the American Tobacco Company, the United Shoe Machinery Company.

No one seemed to want to combine to set high prices. "There was no desire to combine with a view to pushing up the prices," a member of the first cotton combine was reported as saying, "but merely to advance the price a little."[36] Some combiners argued that they were not raising prices at all, merely "stabilizing" or "regulating" them. Others maintained that prices to the consumer had even dropped under combination.[37] The Canadian Canners' Association was congratulated by a Member of Parliament for having formed a combination "not to force up prices, but to get fair prices." And the *Canadian Grocer* once reported that the Wholesale Grocers' Guild had achieved "a restriction on the price of graded sugars to that determined by the open market."[38]

When questioned about safeguards for the consumer in combines arrangements, some restrictionists fell back on their personal sense of duty. The scheme of fixing retail prices on the basis of a 20 per cent mark-up, claimed a member of the executive of the Western Retail Lumbermen's Association (under investigation in 1907 and later prosecuted) had been introduced "with the object of keeping the prices from being excessive to the consumer." As manager of the Association he felt he had "a duty to perform to the public, which is to see that there is no undue advantage taken."[39] Years earlier George Drummond of the Canada Sugar Refinery had made a memorable statement of his sense of public responsibility in response to questioning regarding his superintendency of the Guild's attempts to get what Drummond called "a fair reasonable living advance" on sugar:

Q. It is an agreement as long as you are satisfied with the list?

A. As long as I am satisfied that the thing is being, as I believe it is, honestly and fairly conducted.

Q. Fairly and honestly as between you and the guild?

A. And the public.

Q. Well, the public, according to you, have no say in the matter whatever. Their interests are simply affected as to the advance which you and the guild agree upon, that the sugar must be sold at. The public have no control over the agreement in any way whatever. The agreement is not an agreement between the guild and you and the public, it is an agreement between you and the guild which affects the public. Is that not so?

A. Well, that is a very long question.

Q. Has the public any control over the agreement?

A. Well, you covered that.

Q. I understand the public has no control over the agreement?

A. Well –

Q. Do you say that they have?

A. I don't know; we will see.

Q. I want you to answer that question; I put the question; I would like an answer.

A. I don't think a gentleman should ask a question like that; it is wasting time.[40]

47

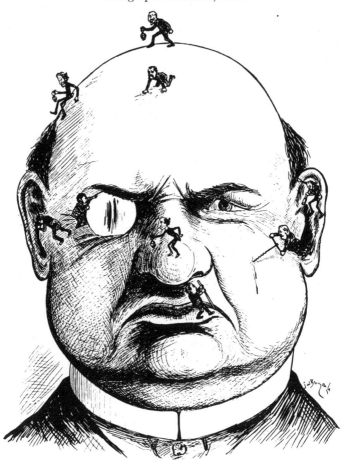

THE GOVERNMENT "INVESTIGATING" MONOPOLY

A more sophisticated defence of profit margins under combines stressed the residual forces of the marketplace. An "unreasonable" advance in prices would be sure to offer opportunities for competitors to step into a field or for the members themselves to violate agreements. Even in 1910 when mergers had given single companies up to 85 per cent of the Canadian market, Fred Field of the *Monetary Times* felt it was still "almost impossible" to prevent competition in a new and growing country. As soon as one company was seen to be operating without restraint, "capital and enterprise will quickly change the situation."[41]

No combine, of course, ever admitted to exorbitant profit-taking. The Wholesale Grocers' Guild maintained that its sugar profits ranged between 2.75 per cent and 4.25 per cent on costs, whereas the accepted average rate of return on wholesale groceries was 4.5 per cent. Well aware that these issues often hinged on the manipulation of statistics, a spokesman for the Guild offered to place a $1,000 cheque in the hands of the mayor of Toronto to be distributed to city charities if his figures were not found to be substantially correct. They were not disputed in the press or by the Select Committee on combines. Others made a less persuasive case. The 20 per cent mark-up allowed by the Western Retail Lumbermen's Association, it turned out, was calculated to provide a 10 per cent net profit on turnover which could produce a 100 per cent annual return on capital.[42]

Restrictionists also claimed that combines served the public by preserving and increasing efficiency. The distribution of sugar through wholesale grocers was the cheapest way of bringing this article to the public, Guild spokesmen claimed. Did the public really want to force the wholesalers to go out of the business and compel the refiners to set up their own expensive distribution system? Was it truly in the public interest to encourage bankers to lend money on unsound principles because of competition, leading nowhere but to impaired capital, disastrous failures, and scandals? After all, said George Hague of the Merchants' Bank, "To lend the community too much money is not beneficial." As trade associations gave way to holding companies and organic mergers in the twentieth century, claims of economies and efficiencies to be gained through consolidation were their most common justification. It was admitted that the formation of the Steel Company of Canada, for example, would end competition among its constituents. But the savings created by lower shipping costs, specialization and longer production runs, and consolidation of the sales force, it was predicted, would allow products to be sold at a lower price ("if necessary") than in the past, but at a larger profit to the company. Most other amalgamations made similar claims.[43]

Alternatively, some members of combines justified their actions by maintaining they prevented the growth of giant enterprises tending to monopoly. Totally free competition, they argued, would lead to the survival of the fittest in the form of either trusts or monopolies. In a campaign to have the Criminal Code changed to legalize small businessmen's combines, the Retail Merchants' Association maintained that the existing anti-combines sections induced the creation of monopolistic corporations by permitting businessmen to combine and fix prices through joint stock companies while prohibiting them from doing the same thing on an individual basis in trade associations. Far better to permit and even encourage the regulation of competition than to foster an end to competition by making sane regulations illegal. After all, the department stores were obviously inaugurated with "the prime motive of destroying your opponents and then creating a monopoly for selfish purposes, and public inconvenience."[44] An eminently respectable academic economist had defended the Wholesale Grocers' Guild for the same reasons in 1890, charging that unrestrained competition would lead to "the destruction of the trading and manufacturing middle class and the growth on its ruins of a few colossal businesses." Accordingly, "the tendency of the combines will, in this respect, seem conservative in the best sense of the word."[45]

Effective regulation of competition hinged on the ability to force would-be mavericks to obey the regulations. This posed the question of commercial liberty in its starkest form (since the outsider was often the victim of boycotts and other discriminatory devices) and was the point at which many otherwise sympathetic observers of the combination movement balked. Responding to the *Monetary Times'* stated belief that the sugar combine's attempts to interfere with third parties could not be tolerated in a country where commerce was free, Hugh Blain, a leading Toronto wholesaler, offered a common defence of coercion in the interests of a majority of traders:

Man's liberty is met in every direction by man's safety. The two stand in juxtaposition to each other. You cannot abnormally increase the one without infringing on the other. Safety so increased gives opportunity for oppression, and liberty so increased becomes a dangerous license. Whichever one of these may be of most consequence to the community should be secured and protected, and if necessary even by an encroachment on the other. The liberty of these individual merchants is curtailed to the extent only, that he or they are required to observe laws voluntarily adopted by nearly all the trade in the general interest, just as a citizen is obliged to obey laws passed by a majority of the voters in the general interests of the community.

To talk of a dangerous violation of man's liberty, and British freedom under such circumstances, seems to me a mere device for popular applause, thoughtless hereditary buncombe, . . . No person will advocate liberty for the ordinary lunatic, especially if dangerous to others. May I ask, why be so solicitous about the liberty of the commercial lunatic?[46]

Businessmen who stayed out of combines, or, worse still, broke free from arrangements they had been a party to, were condemned as commercial mavericks, selfish, unprincipled, and immoral. Price-cutters lacked the courage to "meet rivals on fair ground and succeed"; their business life was "conceived in selfishness and nurtured by methods the very antithesis of business-like."[47] Very probably they were able to cut prices only because they sold inferior goods, exploited their employees, or both. The Retail Merchants' Association never tired of pointing to the low wages and poor working conditions in the department stores and their allied factories. These institutions, it charged, were engaged in "the vicious process of pauperizing labor" (and were also, according to the *Canadian Pharmaceutical Journal,* "the supreme personification of egotism, selfishness, and greed"). Surely the merchant who refused to join an early-closing movement and give his clerks free time to enjoy life, thought *Le Moniteur du Commerce,* "a moins d'égards pour son employé qu'il en aurait pour son cheval ou pour son chien!" By contrast, the men who came together in the new association movement were dedicated to stopping dishonest and unfair competitive practices and were the guardians of business ethics, lifting whole trades onto a new, higher plane of commercial morality. "The old business principles," said T. J. Drummond of the Lake Superior Corporation, "were a distrust of one's competitors, the idea that to succeeed yourself you must thrust out your rivals, and the solid belief that your rivals are mean enough to feel the same way towards you . . . the law of distrust was our basic principle." The new principle, he said, quoting Judge Gary of U. S. Steel, was "I believe what is good for my competitors is good for me."[48]

A final, very significant defence of business collectivism hinged on relating it to other, more socially acceptable forms of combination. Surely the statutes governing the liberal professions were laws giving private groups the right to form combines restricting access and fixing prices in their trades. Why should there be a public hue and cry against combines designed to make sure staple articles were sold at a profit, asked the *Commercial,* but no thought of interfering with the fixed fees of doctors, lawyers, and other professionals, "many of which are a much more flagrant fraud upon the public than has ever been heard of in the field of commerce?" "We meet together the same as doctors do," said a Western lumber dealer defending his combine, "for mutual benefit." The actions taken by the Western Retail Lumbermen's Association to prevent manufacturers from selling to consumers were simply a matter of business ethics, "the same as you may charge some person with violating professional etiquette." Bankers openly preached the doctrine that professionalism in banking meant an end to unwise competition. "If banking is worthy the name of a profession," ran an article in the *Journal of the Canadian Bankers' Association,* "there should be certain things universally considered unprofessional within our ranks. Giving service without profit or at an actual loss should be unprofessional. Solicitation of business by offering to work more cheaply should be as unworthy a banker as we consider it unworthy a doctor."[49]

At the other end of the social scale, workingmen had their own combinations, trade unions. Was there any real difference between a trade combination and a trade union? Referring to the cotton combine of 1886, the *Journal of Commerce* suggested that manufacturing combines were "in aims, powers and results achieved . . . almost identical with those enjoyed by trades unions, though they are seldom endowed with the authority wielded by officials of labor organizations; and as we seldom hear of any evil results to the public at large resulting from the latter associations, it seems idle to fear that the establishment of a body so essentially businesslike as the one in question, can in any way prove prejudicial to public interests." The Canadian Manufacturers' Association was told at its annual meeting in 1889 that the main pressure for laws regulating combines seemed to come from labour organizations, "which in themselves are perhaps the most notable instance of combines on record" because of their attempts to control the labour market. When the anti-combines act of that year was understood to exclude trade unions there were bitter objections in the Senate about class discrimination, and for the next twenty years businessmen argued that the law of combinations should be applied equally: either trade associations should be given the same exemptions as trade unions, or trade unions should have their exemptions removed. It seemed odd that workers should be permitted to combine to achieve a living wage and businessmen forbidden to combine to achieve a living profit.[50]

One reason why the condemnations of competition in business were so frequent was because of the general failure of most attempts to limit it. The failure rate of trade association agreements, combines, and attempts at monopoly was very high. It was inherently difficult to build barriers around a free market. The peculiarity of associational activities among businessmen was that "scabbing" was even more effective in their field than when it was employed against trade unions. A single non-union worker could have little effect breaking a normal strike. A single price-cutting Timothy Eaton or Robert Simpson could demoralize thousands of retailers across the country. A single renegade manufacturer could delight in undoing the most complicated stabilizing arrangements:

What is it that doth shake the trade
And make each grocery man afraid
To buy, lest he may pay too dear,
The fall in prices being near?
  'Tis Brantford Starch.

What is it that doth make Rome howl
And cause the Guild to fight and growl,
And harbor naughty vengeful feelings
Towards the firm who loves fair dealings?
  'Tis Brantford Starch.[51]

Organic mergers leading to oligopoly could ease the competitive problems of some businessmen. As with the early-closing movement and the trading-stamp "evil," governments did occasionally meet the demands of businessmen to have their trade restrictions sanctioned by law. On the whole, though, government attitudes ranged from benign neutrality and the passing of merely ceremonial anti-combines laws through alarming and zealous prosecution of combines by some provincial attorneys-general.[52] Without the force of law behind them, combinations in restraint of trade remained purely voluntary agreements, apt to be shattered at the whim of any enterprising merchant.

Although there were enough of these enterprising individualists in most areas of business to frustrate much of the flight from competition, the strength of resistance to competition by businessmen must not be underrated. In a purely competitive marketplace a businessman had no security, no certainty, no sense of control over his own fate. He could be hard-working, honest, and thrifty, but still find his business and his livelihood destroyed by competitors who were wealthier, more efficient, or less scrupulous. In the real world of business most participants in the market would have amended the formula for material success to read Industry, Integrity, Frugality, and Fixed Prices. The continued freedom of enterprise was a function of the impersonal forces of the marketplace, not of the desires of a majority of traders. In these years the free market survived because businessmen did not have the power to control decisions affecting their livelihood.

Chapter 3

# The Workingman's Welfare

The deceased proved to be a man named John Weimar, a handsome young fellow of twenty-seven who was to have married in a few days. It appears that he had written to his employer, Mr. Limpert, for money then due him, but Mr. Limpert took the occasion to dispense with his services. The prospect of losing his situation on the eve of his marriage seems to have preyed upon his mind, and without considering the trouble to his fiancée, he weakly came to the determination to take his life.

— *Canadian Journal of Fabrics*, 1894

By the 1880s Canadians had begun to discover the social problems and conflicts that seemed everywhere a consequence of the Industrial Revolution. They were already aware of the British experience half a century earlier; it apparently demonstrated that subsistence wages, harsh discipline, and the exploitation of women and children were the dark underside of the coming of the age of factories. Now that the rapid development of Canadian manufacturing through a protective tariff was officially the country's National Policy, governments and middle-class reformers were concerned to minimize the incidence of these abuses in Canada. So, too, were the leaders of the highly vocal Canadian labour movement, spokesmen for both the skilled artisans whose craft unions were now reviving from the debacle of the depression of the 1870s, and for thousands of unskilled workers who, in the middle of the decade, were organized for the first time when the American-born Knights of Labor sowed hundreds of assemblies across Ontario and Quebec. They claimed that Canada was being blighted with dark Satanic mills, that exploitation and hardship were commonplaces of Canadian industrialism, and that public intervention (as well as direct action) was absolutely necessary to protect the welfare of the workingman.

Particularly when petitions were backed with the threat of political action by organized labour, governments responded to these concerns with investigations and legislation. The Royal Commission on the Relations of Labor and Capital, formally established in 1886 and popularly known as the Royal Labor Commission, was a major inquiry into working conditions and wages, taking evidence from some 1800 witnesses in every industrial and commercial centre in central and eastern Canada. Already by the time of its report in 1889 Ontario and Quebec had passed their first Factory Acts to regulate safety conditions, child labour, and hours of work. Although these actions had little significant immediate effect on the welfare of workers, they did mean that employers now had to explain and justify the physical conditions of work in their establishments, the wages they offered to various classes of help, and the hours they expected workers to toil. Employers were being called upon to accept responsibility for their workers' welfare. For many businessmen social insistence on this responsibility came as a considerable shock.

The most sensational revelations of the Royal Labor Commission concerned working conditions in cigar factories in Montreal. Apprentice cigar-makers, boys and girls as young as ten years of age, were being subjected to brutal discipline by factory foremen and owners. In the worst factory, that of J. M. Fortier, the little workers were overseen by a "special constable" employed to keep them at their jobs, imprisoned in a "black hole" in the cellar for misbehaving, and slapped, kicked, and hit by their bosses. The owner himself had once beaten a seventeen-year-old girl for insubordination. In their reports the outraged commissioners recommended that such "barbarous practices" be made a penal offence, "so that Canadians may no longer rest under the reproach that the lash and the dungeon are accompaniments of manufacturing industry in the Dominion." It seemed a totally inexplicable, inhuman exploitation of the helpless.[1]

Not to J. M. Fortier. He testified that most of his young apprentices worked in his factory at the instigation of their parents, had to be watched closely because they were apt to steal tobacco, and were routinely "chastised" and "corrected" in the factory just as they would be disciplined at school or in their homes. The system of corporal punishment in the factory had been authorized by the local police magistrate. The "black hole" was an enclosure under the cellar steps where apprentices committing serious offences were shut in, sometimes instead of being taken to be charged before the magistrate. Fortier would have permitted one of his own daughters to be disciplined, "if she deserved it," in the same way he had disciplined seventeen-year-old Georgina Loiselle (who still worked in the factory five years later, and who, Fortier thought, "is very glad to have received the lesson she did, for she has been an obedient girl ever since then"). He, Fortier, had never been beaten during his apprenticeship, but only because he did not happen to have needed it: "otherwise I should have been." The local magistrate appeared before the commission to reinforce Fortier's testimony, claiming that he too expected his children to be disciplined at school and at home, and a delegation of mothers and older women workers at Fortier's testified that nothing went on there which would not be tolerated in their own homes. If anything, Fortier thought that the work and discipline in his factory was good for his little helpers.[2]

Though an extreme case, Fortier was not untypical of conservative businessmen who could not understand outsiders' criticisms of their employment practices. The members of the Royal Labor Commission, who had interviewed dozens of semi-literate and illiterate boys and girls, many less than fourteen years old, working in textile and saw mills, tobacco and cigar factories across the country, felt that child labour was physically, morally, and intellectually harmful for the children. The men who employed the children, though, denied that the work had any harmful effects or that they were specially responsible for the children having to work. The work was always light, they claimed, and was good for children because "the having to be neat, industrious, and obedient, ... goes far towards making them valuable citizens, and in building up a country."[3] In an age when compulsory education laws were non-existent or unenforced, the alternative to working children would be idle children, loafing about the streets, learning bad habits, and, as a manufacturer complained in a private C.M.A. meeting, "subject to all the demoralizing influences of the localities in which they were forced to live." In any case, some of the employers themselves had been whipped into line in the mines or gone into the textile mills as twelve year olds.[4]

More to the point, businessmen placed most of the blame for child labour on parents. Young children were as much of a bother as their work was worth, employers complained, and sometimes it was more trouble to keep them out of the mills than keeping them in. The manager of the Merchants' Cotton Company explained his problem to the Royal Labor Commission this way:

A man will be working at the mill, and his daughter working there also, and he may have a small child, whom he desires to have there, for instance, in the spooling room. Often you don't want to take the child, but if you do not, he and his daughter will go out, and they will go to some mill where the whole three will be employed. . . .

When girls come to the mill their mothers often come with them, and beg the chance of getting them on to work. For instance, there was a mother brought a girl the other day. I said she was small. The mother replied, "I went into the mill about that age." I told her the terms on which we took hands, and that at first she would get very little pay. She replied that she understood that, and she knew where she was going to start. She told me the particulars of her own case, and how she had worked up until she was able to get good pay.[5]

Other employers called for a strengthening of the truancy laws, and after legislation regulating child labour was introduced they complained to factory inspectors that parents encouraged children to lie about their age.[6] They also wondered whether an increase in the age limit at which children could work would not cause "a great deal of hardship, as many children who worked were the sole support of widowed mothers or invalid parents."[7]

Rigid discipline in work-places – fines, locked doors, withheld pay, searches, etc. – was justified on the grounds of workers' tendencies to lateness, absenteeism, inattention to their machines, and shoddy effort. "I simply says this [sic]," the owner of a St. Hyacinthe knitting mill testified, "unless there is a certain amount of discipline in a factory where two hundred hands are employed you cannot run it." And a foreman in a Sherbrooke cigar manufactory explained the special problems of managing the young:

. . . it is not any easy thing to run a factory where the employees are largely composed of young people, and you must have some system. Now, the moment your back is turned, it may be, three or four of the hands will jump up and commence to knock each other down, and have, what they consider, a good time. If this kind of thing is allowed the material is wasted, and the machinery or plant may be broken. If you were to step out for a few minutes and were to step in again, and find three or four of the leading spirits jumping up and laughing, etc., and encouraging the others to do the same, you would be ready to order them to leave the factory. The rule is there for the purpose of preserving order, and not with the view of being harsh to them.[8]

Some employers also found it difficult to understand the need for improved safety conditions in their establishments. It had been normal to assume that a worker who took a job accepted the risks that went along with it. If he had an accident – getting his hand caught in an unguarded machine, for example, or falling down an unbarricaded lift shaft – then he had been negligent or careless. It was standard testimony before the Royal Labor commission that machinery was not in itself dangerous, that the men's own carelessness brought on accidents, or that they had known of the hazards when they took the job. Railway executives, for example, agreed that coupling freight cars by hand and running along their tops to apply brakes could be hazardous occupations, especially in bad weather. Brakemen frequently did fall from cars, a superintendent admitted, "but not where the men are looking where they are going, . . . I claim that where men take the responsibility on themselves the railway companies are not to blame." According to Thomas Shaughnessy, C.P.R. investigations showed accidents seldom happened to new employees, who were naturally careful, but were much more common to men "who have become careless from long experience, and who take chances that necessarily result in their meeting with an accident sooner or later." As late as 1909 mine operators found it near heresy for a young turk in the industry to lay most of the blame for accidents on the failure of management to enforce safety rules. "The miner, as a rule, is naturally negligent," was the response to his paper from members of the Canadian Mining Institute.[9]

The most common response to pressures to improve sanitation and ventilation within factories (aside from the claim that conditions were already very advanced) was that the workers themselves did not desire the changes. A young iron foundryman, Edward Gurney, told the Royal Labor Commission that he had thought he should be up-to-date and do well for his iron moulders by providing them with washing-up rooms:

> but my experience was so disastrous that I lost faith in that sort of thing, and I registered a mighty oath I never would do any such foolishness as that again. When I built the present foundry I built a room (against the opinion of my father, who had more knowledge of such things than I), so that the men might have a place to wash in. I fitted it up with warm and cold water and everything of that kind. The men would not go there; they washed in the pots in the foundry, as they always had done, and as their fathers did before them. I got well laughed at, and by none more so than by the men.[10]

Other employers complained to factory inspectors about employees who were indifferent to improvements in surroundings or who despoiled and mutilated shiny new washrooms and lunchrooms. They also complained that workingmen would remove guards they had placed on machinery. Some saw little reason why factories should be injurious to the health of employees who breathed less pure air and had less ventilation in their homes than were provided at their work-places. And it was difficult to understand why the Royal Commissioners of the 1880s wanted water-closets installed in coal mines ("there is always plenty of places in the old workings out of the main workings") or why employers should install fire-escapes when government buildings did not have them, ventilate their workrooms better than schools were ventilated, or install running water and flush toilets in towns that had no sewage systems.[11] Referring to ventilation, a government study in the early 1880s had reported that "While this question of such vital importance to humanity, is being treated with indifference by the authorities of churches, halls, and our public schools, it certainly cannot be a matter of surprise that manufacturers do not take the lead of equally responsible parties on this question, or that they should be forced to an expenditure which the State, under similar circumstances, does not provide for its subjects."[12]

Nor could many employers understand why there should now have to be questions asked about the hours employees worked. David Morrice, the Montreal cotton lord, thought two legal holidays a year for the hands of the Hochelaga Cotton Company were quite sufficient. In addition to Sundays they had Saturday afternoons off. "I work a great deal longer myself, I can assure you." Frederic Nicholls, secretary of the Canadian Manufacturers' Association, thought it "difficult" to judge what the proper hours of work should be, only knowing that he put in sixteen in his business every day (he allowed that he was not physically capable of sixteen hours of heavy physical work, but wondered if physical labour was always the hardest). In 1907 a manufacturer Member of Parliament opposed legislation to limit working hours with the claim, "If there are any men in this country who work long hours it is the employers of labor, because while the workingman commences work at seven o'clock and quits at six and has his evening to himself, his employer is worried in his office very often until midnight endeavoring to provide the money which enables him to employ labor." Another way of countering demands for shorter hours was to use farm labour as a basis of comparison. Considering the eight-hour movement in the 1880s, the *Monetary Times* recalled the experience of the pioneers:

*–A manufacturers' comment on the implications of limiting hours of work.*

## Some Aspects of the Eight Hour Day Movement

THE
FISHERMAN  "HI, DROP THAT NET, TIME'S UP.
THIS IS AN EIGHT HOUR BOAT"

THE HIRED MAN
"CAN'T HELP IT IF IT IS GOIN' TO RAIN, IT'S
FIVE MINUTES OVER MY TIME AND I'M
GOIN' TO QUIT."

THE DOCTOR

"I'LL COME BACK AND
FINISH YOU TOMORROW. THE UNION'LL BE AFTER
ME IF I DON'T STOP WHEN THE WHISTLE BLOWS."

A commission in Nova Scotia is investigating the conditions of labor
with special reference to the establishment of a general eight
hour work day

... it was the custom of the country to work from sunrise to sunset. Farmers expected their hired men to work the same hours, and they only asked them what they were willing to do themselves. It was these long hours that carved the farms out of the forest, and in the farmer's case, winter gave no rest; he pursued his cheerful toil from year's end to year's end, his eye steadily set on that independence which was the darling object of his life.

Fighting bills to establish the eight-hour day on public works twenty years later, the Canadian Manufacturers' Association regularly alerted agricultural papers to the implications of a shorter day for farm work, knowing they would get the support of rural M.P.'s.[13]

Some employers thought that workers would only waste a shorter working day or higher pay. The business press reported that nine-tenths of Chicago workers on the eight-hour day spent their extra time in saloons, and that English workers on high pay had bought silks and satins and hothouse fruits instead of saving their money. What would happen, asked the *Journal of Commerce* in 1893, if the average worker were given more pay than he needed, or more leisure "beyond what can be used up in sleeping and eating?" He would fill the hiatus "with that which commends itself to him as the best satisfaction for vague longings and voids, besides offering the readiest means for disposing of surplus cash, viz., drink. It saves a deal of thought." *Le Moniteur du Commerce* posed the problem very well by asking whether Canadian workingmen were ready to take advantage of extra leisure:

Sera-t-ce pour le repos, ou pour l'amusement ou pour un autre genre de travail: l'instruction par example? Si c'est pour le repos, parfait; si c'est pour s'instruire très bien encore; mais pour l'amusement, nous avons des craintes; car les tentations mauvaises sont nombreuses pour notre jeunesse et à part quelques exceptions bien faciles à compter, les moyens de distraction soit disant honnête que nous possédons sont d'une monotonie désésperante et généralement d'une fadeur à faire lever le coeur au plus blasé. Le danger est qu'un changement trop brusque ne suprenne nos gens au point de leur faire oblier qu'ils doivent ménager leurs forces pour le travail qui est la loi essentielle pour tout homme, qu'il soit ouvrier ou qu'il ne le soit pas.[14]

It is clear that employers were basing these fears and objections on a stereotype of workers as naturally undisciplined, lazy, and inclined to dissipate their energy and wages. It was flaws in the character of workingmen – unwillingness to work or save or educate themselves – which held them back, not any failure of the system. As the manager of a Cape Breton colliery told the Royal Labor Commission, "There are men in the mines who have money in the bank and are comfortably off, while there are others who have the same wages who have no money and are in debt. Their money goes into the pockets of the rum sellers."[15]

The best expression of this individualist notion of self-help – the idea that the sufficient prescription for the worker's welfare was for him to be industrious, honest, and thrifty – was an 1894 address by George Hague, general manager of the Merchants' Bank, to the Y.M.C.A., entitled *Some Practical Considerations on the Subject of Capital and Labor.* Arguing that legislative interference with working hours would violate natural law and create unearned wages and leisure, Hague believed the only effective and Christian solution to the labour problem was to reform "*the character of each individual.*" Referring back to the England of thirty years ago, he instanced those workers who regularly spent a high percentage of their earnings on luxuries – drink, tobacco, and sport – and kept Monday as a holiday, "Saint Monday," yet declaimed by the hour about their political and social grievances. "Instead of blaming themselves, and seeking to reform their own character, they blamed the organization of society and Government for the condition in which they lived, and were loud in their demands for more freedom, more wages, more leisure, and more of the good things of life generally, all to be furnished at the expense of other people." In the same town, though, there were thousands of "God-fearing, church-attending, industrious, sober and thrifty" workmen whose homes were respectable, clean, and orderly, and whose children were well brought up and comfortable. "Eschewing the baneful luxuries of drink, tobacco and gambling, these men had the real luxuries of a good home, a balance in the Savings Bank, a place in the Church, and a good prospect for old age." There was no need, Hague concluded, for any "organized schemes" for the betterment of workingmen, only for men to become sober, industrious, and respectable by making Christianity a vital force in their lives. The maxims that would lead to success for an aspiring young businessman were equally applicable to aspiring young workers.[16]

In this individualistic system the employer had done his part in contributing to the worker's welfare when he offered a man a job, and had done a little bit more when he provided work for the man's wife and children. The employer provided men with wages (why sympathize with operatives in the cotton industry, the *Journal of*

*Commerce* said, "a portion of the population, who, previous to the recent establishment of the various factories were not worth twenty-five cents a day, but who now are worth from seventy-five cents to $1.25 a day, adding thus much to their value to the country?") and with an opportunity to put their skill and ambition to work and make something of themselves. It was always assumed that employers would reward good and faithful service: "he would not be a true business man if those who assisted him to obtain such advantages did not also reap some benefit therefrom by sharing in the increased profits of the business."[17]

In any case, employers pleaded that in a competitive economy they could not afford changes in the conditions of work because cost increases would price them out of their markets. At one time or another every suggestion made by the members of the Royal Labor Commission was met with pleas that competition would not permit changes. Child labour and low wages were necessary in the textile industries to compete with the Americans and British. Quebec manufactories had to work on religious holidays to compete with Ontario factories. Ontario cigar-makers could not raise wages if they were to compete with the Quebec industry. On a national level too high costs of production, arising from an eight-hour day, for example, would nullify the effects of the tariff and price Canadian products out of their market, let alone the export markets manufacturers were hoping to cultivate. "A nation that resolves to labor less than its rivals will produce less, and in the world's competition must go to the wall," pontificated the *Monetary Times*. "Its artisans, in losing hold on the world's markets, would lose their bread. . . . Not by such expedients can a nation find the way to wealth or comfort."[18]

In the meantime workers should realize the hazards employers endured in the provision of jobs. In the hard world of business it was the employer who risked losing everything while the workers collected wages at no risk at all. Capitalists, said *Industrial Canada*, were "the men who are slaving night and day to give the men employment," often going for years without profits or dividends, while the men themselves were becoming affluent and insolent on their steady pay. Or, as the *Journal of Commerce* tried to explain to ignorant clergymen who believed workers should have a share of profits,

> . . . between the position of the employer and the employed there is a radical difference. The employer puts into an enterprise his capital, his experience, his business skill. He ventures

**Workman:** "There's the old man counting up his money as usual."

A closer inspection shows that that is just what "the old man" is doing.

these on very treacherous waters. After long years of struggling, of keenest anxiety, and of labors most exhausting, he often finds himself bereft of his capital, his strength and his energy, he is bankrupt and broken-hearted when too old to have any hope or chance to recover his position. During all those years those he employed have drawn their wages week in and week out, they took no risks, their sleep was never destroyed by anxiety over trade troubles, and when the master is ruined and his capital gone, they do not share in his misfortunes. Indeed, often times saving men during the whole period in which their master has been going down hill to ruin, have been going up hill to a certain competency. On what principle of equity then can those who run none of the risks of a business expect to share in its profits?[19]

These were the elements of the rigid, conservative response to charges that an employer had a responsibility for his workers' welfare, a virtually total denial of responsibility. Although it was the bias towards which most businessmen's opinions tended, there were also currents of sympathy with the problems of the workingman and expressions of outrage at the more glaring injustices reported in the press and uncovered in investigations. When a Royal Commission exposed horrendous working conditions during the construction of the Crow's Nest Pass Railway, for example, the *Monetary Times* deplored "the grossly brutal and inhuman treatment of the men," damned the C.P.R. for its negligence, and called for government supervision of working conditions on all future subsidized lines. Earlier the *Canadian Manufacturer* had supported Toronto's initiation of a minimum wage on city contracts, agreeing that no one in Canada should work for less than fifteen cents an hour, had found it barbarous that Quebec law should still permit imprisonment for debt, and had decried the sweating conditions in the Toronto garment trade uncovered by Mackenzie King in a series of articles in the *Mail and Empire*. It had referred to the "outrageous oppression" found in Montreal cigar factories by the Royal Labor Commission, and seven years later referred to J. M. Fortier as "the girl spanker." The only business paper to comment on the Fortier affair in detail, *Le Moniteur du Commerce,* labelled it "une énormité, et un scandale . . . contre lesquels on ne saurait trop hautement protester." It rightly blamed the Quebec Masters and Servants Act, against which it had been protesting for several years ("détestable dans ses termes et indigne d'un peuple civilisé"), along with the feudal ideas of the police magistrate, and called for inspection "sévère" of child labour in factories.[20]

The best example of the willingness of businessmen to see obvious grievances remedied was their position on factory legislation when this important issue of public control of business was first raised in the 1880s. The *Monetary Times* expected manufacturers to oppose factory legislation, but was impressed by the way it had worked in England and felt that fears of injustice to manufacturers should be subordinated to "the higher interests of life and health." It agreed with the Toronto Trades' Council's programme: factory acts and employers' liability laws were of special interest to workingmen, "and justice and humanity cannot refuse to grant them." In fact manufacturers did not oppose factory legislation, having realized from the beginning of the discussion that, as the secretary of the C.M.A. told the members, it would be both "inevitable" and useful as "the regulator and balance wheel" of the industrial system. No one could deny that employment abuses would develop in Canada as they had in England or that the state had a right to intervene to protect the helpless. Although manufacturers did worry that too stringent regulations might hurt their competitive position (and for this reason were strong supporters of national factory legislation) and actively lobbied to limit factory inspectors' powers to dictate changes, they at no time adopted an antediluvian stand against the right of the state to guarantee the safety of all workers and to protect the helpless.[21]

Further, employers like J. M. Fortier who would make no concession to non-pecuniary claims on their humanity were balanced by others whose paternal interest in their workers and economic interest in avoiding labour problems involved them in voluntary attempts to improve their hands' position. The Royal Labor Commission was pleased to interview Douglas Rutherford, a Montreal contractor who, twenty years earlier, had broken the prevailing custom of reducing wages in winter: "when the right time comes and I find that I can increase the men's wages without request on their part I do so, and by that system we have avoided strikes and difficulties of all sorts." George Tuckett, a Hamilton tobacco manufacturer, had voluntarily shortened his employees' working day and found they worked better because of it. He also gave annual bonuses, having found "they notice we are watching their interests and rewarding merit; and therefore they watch our interests." It happened that Tuckett's hands were organized and had obtained a number of benefits since organization; but, as one of them testified, "we have not the least doubt he would have done it before we had been organized. . . . He is a very good man to work for." Zephirin Paquette, Quebec City merchant and manufacturer, had a policy of employing no one under sixteen among his 250 operatives, paid extra wages for overtime work, and took pride in never having had disputes with his workers "other than may occur among the members of a well-conducted family."[22]

Employers like these were trying to maintain the personal relationship of master and man into the age of large enterprises. Companies carried on traditions of socializing: picnics and outings, dances, and presentations of gifts by masters to men and vice versa. In 1882, for example, the proprietor of the North American Rubber Company gave a ball for his 125 employees who responded by presenting him and the manager with portraits in oil. They were jointly celebrating having had a full year's work to do for the first time since the factory opened. In the same year George Smith celebrated the enlargement of his woollen factory at Lambton Mills by entertaining his hundred workers at a garden tea party in his house, followed by "a great musical and literary treat" in the new factory. Bennett Rosamond, textile patriarch of Almonte, Ontario, and an ex-president of the C.M.A., threw a traditional Christmas party for his employees, featuring a supper, dancing, songs by the mill choir, and a Christmas tree stocked with presents for the children. Lumber magnate John Waldie wrote to Sir Wilfrid Laurier in 1898 describing "the pleasure and enjoyment" he had in giving a Christmas turkey to each family in his employ and a $5.00 gold piece to each baby. In an example of classic paternalism, J. R. Booth, "the Chaudière Carnegie," paid his men $12,000 in unearned wages during the Grand Trunk strike of 1910 instead of laying them off. They decided to honour him and sent for their employer. The *Canada Lumberman*'s account of the incident is a memorable picture of benevolent feudalism:

The message to Mr. Booth asked him to attend at 12 o'clock at the mill.... Mr. Booth sent word that he would be on hand a little before 1 o'clock. He preferred not to interfere with the men's eating time.

The lumber king reached the yard by a back route and was on a high lumber wagon looking down at 1,000 happy men before many of them noticed him. Those who had seen him climb up on the load of pine wondered at the vigor and sprightliness of fourscore years. The kind regards of the mill men were conveyed to Mr. Booth by one of the mill crew.

The lumber king replied in a simple and direct style. He said: "Gentlemen, it is a pleasure to me to see that you are so thankful for the little I have done for you.

"It was this way. I felt that I could stand the loss better than you could (Cheers). I was sorry for you, but that alone would not have brought you bread and butter. . . .

"Now, gentlemen, I was sorry for you, and sorry to the extent of $12,000 (Prolonged applause).

"Besides the wages, I lose by this strike another $12,000 or $15,000 as the result of interference with business. Yet I am heartily repaid for it all by hearing you men express your thanks to me."[23]

It was also often realized that high wages and good working conditions produced contented workers. As early as 1880 the *Monetary Times* was drawing attention to the connection between ventilation, cleanliness, and the health of workers, suggesting that healthy, contented workers were more productive. The *Canadian Manufacturer* argued that reducing a man "almost to the level of a machine" would lead to dissatisfaction with the job, an attitude of trying to do the least amount of work in a given time. "On the other hand, if the workman feels comfortable in his work, and if he be stimulated by due appreciation and hope of fair reward for useful improvements, then the feeling of comfort and energy of thought will show themselves in increased skill and carefulness and greater diligence." Firms that installed advanced safety and ventilation systems, dining rooms for their hands, clubrooms, or other recreational facilities were often noticed and praised in the business press. In such early company towns as Marysville, New Brunswick, Walkerville, Ontario, Valleyfield and Capelton in Quebec, it was common for employers to assume responsibilities well beyond the weekly payroll – providing housing, municipal services, playgrounds, etc. If only because company towns initially had to draw workers from other localities, their facilities had to be at least marginally superior to existing conditions. The deterioration and complaints about exploitive paternalism would set in later.[24]

In the decade before World War I older approaches to employee welfare developed into the more formalized "welfare work" or "industrial betterment" movement. In tune with a more organized and more extensive movement in the United States, a number of Canadian factories were now introducing bath and shower rooms, kitchens and lunchrooms, experimenting with mutual benefit societies and monthly magazines, while continuing the old standbys of annual excursions, Christmas turkeys, and retirement bonuses. *Industrial Canada* carried regular articles extolling those factories that had gone in for welfare work, advocating improvements in lighting and ventilation, personalized lockers for workingmen, turning heaps of ugly brick into "the factory beautiful," and supporting movements afoot in

Toronto to provide better housing for the working class.[25] By 1913 the Toronto Branch of the Canadian Manufacturers' Association had launched the first sizable low-cost housing project in Canada and in 1910 had raised $25,000 to help the Y.W.C.A. found model working girls' houses.[26] Canadian railway companies, at first much more reluctant than their American counterparts, now gave enthusiastic support to the "railway work" of the Y.M.C.A., funding "Railway Associations" that provided the usual range of Y.M.C.A. activities. The Canadian Reading Camp Association, predecessor of Frontier College, had twenty-five reading rooms in operation in lumber camps by 1904, also funded by employers, and was beginning to spread into mining camps.[27]

By the turn of the century the largest Canadian corporations, banks and railways, were introducing formal pension plans for their employees. These were consciously seen as a way of increasing employee morale and affection for the firm. Now a man would know he would be looked after in his declining years as a matter of right, not charity. In 1902, Thomas Shaughnessy explained the C.P.R.'s purpose in introducing its pension scheme: "The company hopes, by thus voluntarily establishing a system under which a continued income will be assured to those who after years of continuous service are by age or infirmity no longer fitted to perform their duties, and without which they might be left without means of support, to build up amongst them a feeling of permanency in their employment, an enlarged interest in the company's welfare, and a desire to remain in and to devote their best efforts and attention to the company's service." There is also some evidence suggesting that white-collar employees had commonly been provided for in their declining years; when two dry goods houses liquidated their businesses and abandoned their employees in 1893 the *Canadian Journal of Fabrics* protested vigorously against "a selfish and wicked ... precedent, one that is humiliating to the character of the trade."[28]

Businessmen had always been interested in proposals for worker education. In the early years of the twentieth century the Canadian Manufacturers' Association conducted a persistent, well-financed campaign to have established a national system of technical education. The motivation behind the scheme was, of course, complex. Manufacturers were eager to improve their competitive position by having the skills of Canadian workers improved at the state's expense, but were also sincerely interested in elevating the workingman, or rather re-elevating him to artisan status, ending the alienation some employers understood to be a part of the factory system. On this theme one manufacturer went as far as quoting Hegel on the need for personal fulfillment: "The great German philosopher Hegel says: 'This is the absolute right of personal existence – to find itself satisfied in its activity and labor. If men are to interest themselves for anything, they must, so to speak, have part of their existence involved in it; find their individuality gratified by its attainment.'"[29]

It was similarly impossible to disentangle the motives of those businessmen who promoted welfare work. When the Toronto Branch Executive of the C.M.A. discussed workingmen's housing in 1906 the chief advocate of the plan deplored "the miserable conditions under which workingmen were sometimes called to live" and "pointed out the importance to the manufacturer of having a contented lot of workmen," but was also concerned about the need to keep the cost of living low so that manufacturers could keep wages down to meet foreign competition. The Toronto Branch gave its approval to the concept of welfare work, not only because of the "advantage of the employees" that would ensue, but also because when properly carried out it would be "a money making proposition for the employer." It was commonly argued that welfare work would be both humanitarian and profitable because happy workers produced more. At the least, "the intelligent manufacturer of to-day ... knows ... that human beings, like machines, give best service, and require less time and expense for repair when carefully treated, and that good ventilation, wholesome food, and wise recreation are as necessary for the efficiency of the individuals in his employ as are oil and brush for the machinery."\*[31] There were also, of course, the anti-union implications of some forms of paternalism; these are discussed in Chapter 4.

In general businessmen were pleased to see signs of advancement and improved well-being on the part of their workers. "He indeed would not only be a bold but a bad man who regarded the gradual advance of the laboring class from a condition of indigence and oppressive anxiety and domestic discomfort to a state less degrading, with any other feeling than that of satisfaction and thankfulness." For the most part businessmen thought they were seeing improvements in the lot of the workers, in fact a very substantial measure of well-being. When the *Monetary*

---

\*    This mode of arguing was an attempt to appeal to the everyday categories in which businessmen understood their work; it did not imply an inhuman view of the worker as machine. In other articles, businessmen were urged to view their own health in the same terms, to see themselves "as important and valuable as a contropation [*sic*] of brass and steel."

*Times* sent a correspondent to the colliery town of Springhill expecting to find "evidences of squalor, recklessness and unthrift," he instead found "clear proofs of progress and taste," a town with a "clean, roomy, breezy look," and operatives of the mines who were "tidy, industrious, and as different as possible from the Lancashire miners of the Sunday-school books." In 1888 a business editor went to watch the Montreal Labor Day parade, prepared by the rhetoric of labour "agitators" to witness "poverty, patched clothing, and the bent form of the half-fed toiler." Instead,

> ... it must have been truly gratifying to those who really have the welfare of the masses at heart to notice that every man in the procession gave distinct evidence of not only possessing the means of procuring the necessities of life but also a very fair share of its luxuries. An American spectator pointed out that even the poorest sections were well dressed, and that two out of every three wore jewellery of some description. In fact every man present was fully up to the standard of those ordinarily seen in more pretentious gatherings. No poverty was apparent – on the surface at all event – and it looked as if all present not only were in the possession of money to spend but were accustomed to handle it freely.
>
> The truth is (if labor agitators would permit us to recognize the fact) that the average working man has never been so well off as he is at the present day.[32]

Protectionist manufacturers naturally attributed the affluence of Canadian workers to the tariff. As is discussed in Chapter 5, they saw the National Policy as the guarantor of extraordinary prosperity to all Canadians, especially workingmen:

> When the Canadian workman arises in the morning and pulls on a good suit of clothes, enjoys a hearty breakfast of bread and butter and beef and coffee and pastry, all of which are cheaper here than in any part of Europe, and his appetite is stimulated by nice clean china ware instead of the pewter plates of free trade times; and he fills his dinner bucket with good, substantial food, and returns at night to a comfortable home of his own; and his children, as they climb up on his knee tell him in their merry, prattling way what they have learned at free school; and after partaking of a good supper, he picks up the daily paper and posts himself upon the news of the day, then retires to a bed of ease and comfort, he thanks benign providence from the innermost recesses of his

heart that he is permitted to pay even 20 per cent more for everything he buys, so that he may earn 100 per cent more than he could in any other country.

Years later, after the sustained expansion of the Laurier years, it seemed even more obvious that bothersome changes in the Canadian way of economic organization were totally unnecessary. "Considering that we Canadians have attained the good life to a greater degree than most other nations, that our people of all classes are sharing in a uniform prosperity, that we have approached so near to true democracy, where opportunities and rewards are fairly distributed and where all citizens have it within their power to live in comfort and comparative independence, why should there arise a desire to change existing economic conditions, upon which all these are based?"[33]

Most Canadian businessmen thought the worker's material welfare was being adequately served without the presence of unions. Nothing had worsened since the coming of the National Policy factories. Things were as good as or better than they had ever been. Businessmen were impressed by the evidence of New World affluence in Canada. They thought that by virtue of the employment they offered and the attitudes they were instilling in their workers – industry, integrity, thrift – they were already in the vanguard of progress. Surely the opportunities for thrifty and industrious workers to prosper were greater than ever before. True, some tinkering and adjustments in the system were necessary from time to time, a factory act here, divided water-closets and a fire-escape there; businessmen too had been horrified by the pictures of the Lancashire miners in the Sunday-school books. On the whole, though, the system was working well. Therefore it is not surprising that the intrusion of trade unions with their demands for drastic change, their rhetoric of conflict and distrust, and their destructive insistence on having their own way, was met with shock, alarm, and hostility.

Chapter 4

# Unions

The tyranny of trades-unionism is simply damnable.

*— Canadian Manufacturer*, 1889

The brutality of the untamed savage is about labour yet.

*— Journal of Commerce*, 1911

With a few exceptions business comment on trade unions from the first posing of the "labor question" in the 1880s was overwhelmingly hostile. True, businessmen had learned enough to disavow the George Brown die-hard position: the legalization of trade unions in 1872 was accepted as a *fait accompli* all through the period. Business discussions of the labour question proceeded from and were often preceded by the assumption that the right of men to refuse work except on certain terms was as sacred as the right of employers to refuse to hire men except on certain terms. But admitting that men had an abstract "right" to form unions and go on strike was far from accepting the idea of collective bargaining with its implication of equal power positions between capital and labour. Business comment not only stopped well short of approving collective bargaining; it usually stopped short of accepting any of the implications of working-class organization. To most businessmen who articulated their feelings about trade unions these organizations were unnatural and dangerous growths on the economic system, forged from ignorance and/or misunderstanding by a small, irresponsible elite. Their activities were not in the public interest, in the interests of industrial progress and prosperity, or even in the true interests of the working class itself.

The exceptions are worth noting. There were, of course,

employers who had come to terms with unions. They seldom contributed to discussions of the labour question, most undoubtedly having recognized unions against their will. A few unionized employers did express satisfaction with their labour relations, usually claiming that a trade union could instill good sense and discipline in the workers. A C.P.R. superintendent, for example, pointed out that belonging to a union meant an improvement in the men's habits: "I know of several cases of men who have been poor workmen or disgracing themselves have been disciplined by their orders. Lots of the labour unions are very strict on that. They will not have in their union men of intoxicating habits of excess." Other employers stressed the way unions worked to suppress grievances, the union's own committee weeding out frivolous or unreasonable complaints before they reached management.[1] In Cape Breton, the Dominion Coal Company appreciated the "cautious wisdom" of the Provincial Workingman's Association, and "gladly recognize the utility of the P.W.A. as a means of dealing with their men as a body, and as a channel for the proper representation of grievances." It was perhaps significant that this was said in the context of the P.W.A. not having a closed shop at the collieries, never having struck Dominion Coal, and being threatened in its jurisdiction by the militant United Mine Workers of America.[2]

Another current of sympathy with unions flowed from the reactions of some Canadian businessmen to the growth of large-scale industrial organization, particularly in the United States. Some commentators whose ideas of business were formed in an age of small shops and commercial houses occasionally saw clearly what was happening to the old harmony of the artisan's shop. "The decay of domestic industry has well-nigh severed the bonds of sympathy that had from time immemorial united master and man," the *Monetary Times* editorialized in 1896: "Under the factory system, many employers fail to recognize an essential difference between machines and the human labor by which they are operated; kindly interest and consistent devotion have been replaced by indifference and distrust. The outcome has been strikes, lockouts and riots." The development of the corporation, according to the *Commercial,* had broken "the strong chain of mutual dependence" of the old system, creating a situation in which the labourer "is brought face to face with an employer without individuality, without heart, and without moral reputation to lose" and had consequently formed his own powerful, soulless counter-organizations. It felt that the London dock workers had justice on their side in fighting companies organized without hearts, "like Frankenstein's monster," and that the Knights of Labor were acting laudably in battling railways, street-car companies, and other such corporations "as are notorious for the illiberal if not harsh manner in which they treat the laborer."[3]

At various times Canadian business papers condemned the "childish" and "blind" obstinacy of American anthracite coal operators in refusing to recognize unions, predicted that the "oppression and bad management" of English mine owners would eventually create a social and political revolution in that country, deplored the shooting down of unarmed strikers in Pennsylvania, and characterized the use of Pinkerton mercenaries in the Homestead strike as a blot on civilization and the evocation of Lynch law.[4] Although it was easiest to throw stones at other people's glass houses, there were also cases in Canada where employers who took a stand on principle or meanness seemed to go too far. *Le Prix Courant* usually held no brief for unions, but thought the Grand Trunk was displaying "une mesquinerie déplairée et un entêtement injustifiable" in an 1893 freight-handlers strike. The *Monetary Times*, on many issues the most liberal business journal, did not think it was particularly wise or reasonable of an Ottawa lumber firm to precipitate a strike by reducing wages and raising hours to eleven a day in 1893, found that the company policies leading up to rioting at the Sault in 1903 were the limits of "fatuity," and advised the C.P.R. in 1908 that "the friends of the company" would be pleased if its striking shopworkers should not bear the suffering of losing their pension rights. In 1888 the *Journal of Commerce* was outraged at the use of infantry to suppress starving, swindled workmen building the Hereford Railway. The *Canadian Mining Journal*, intensely hostile to the United Mine Workers' strike at Glace Bay in 1909, could not believe that Springhill's Cumberland Coal and Railway Company, which had experienced twenty-two strikes in twenty years, was completely free of blame for the twenty-third, even if the U.M.W.A. was involved.[5]

The good sense of business observers was such that they would not attempt to justify every extremism in labour relations. Nonetheless, the trade-union movement was too powerful, too disruptive of established ways of doing things, too erratic in its early days, its strikes too expensive, and its activities far too close to home for businessmen to preserve a particularly detached position on the labour question. Almost all business comment on unions was critical. The closest to a balanced judgement that most businessmen would have agreed with was the conclusion of a 1909

*Industrial Canada* article: "Unionism undoubtedly is a good thing, in some ways, but like strychnine, it must be taken in small doses."[6]

One almost offhanded way of dismissing the trade union movement, most popular during the 1880s, was to point out that the whole effort of organized labour involved a futile attack on immutable natural law. "The law of supply and demand is a natural law," W. K. McNaught proclaimed, "and trades unions might as well ask the sun to consent to rise in the west and set in the east as to expect that they can by any combination effect any radical change in its workings." Supply and demand was one of the "eternal laws of economy," whose "inevitable" operation could only be "temporarily obstructed" by even the most powerful labour combinations.[7] Statements like these were at once justifications for resistance to labour activity ("the effectual crushing of any organization of that class is a stride made in the direction of free and unfettered trade"[8]) and an affirmation of hope that the union movement would go away. One "encouraging feature" of trade depressions was that the law of supply and demand started reasserting itself again and the workingman came to realize that it was his employer, not his union, who buttered his bread.[9]

More specifically, there was always the defence that the acceptance of unions would raise costs of production to noncompetitive levels, killing "the goose that lays the golden egg." While it might be comparatively easy for unions to frustrate the laws of supply and demand in a local labour market, there was no easy way of interdicting the competition of other producers in other cities, provinces, or countries. Suppose the boss's claim that a wage increase or a strike would force him out of business turned out to be the truth? Suppose the boss got fed up and threatened to pack up his machines and move them somewhere where workers did not bite the hand that fed them and would let a man price his goods competitively? When Senator Sanford's manufacturing company in Hamilton threatened to do this, "the employees of the company were panic stricken, and accepted without a murmur a considerable cut in wages."[10] These were in real life the most effective objections to organized labour, for not until trade unions and government would insist on examining the books of employers could the genuineness of predictions of imminent disaster through higher costs be determined with any accuracy.

Yet in their writing Canadian businessmen seemed reluctant to fall back on arguments stressing the difficulties of competition, both because of the tariff and because of their own considerable interest in limiting competition in the home market. Their analysis of the trade-union movement most commonly concentrated on more direct and personal objections to the effects of unions on the worker and his employer.

They objected strongly to the concept of equality implicit in union demands for standard pay scales and fixed hours of work. Surely these rested on the false assumption that all workers had equal ability and equal motivation. "The weakest point of these Unions is that they demand that their members shall all be paid the same wages, good, bad and indifferent, it makes no matter, the pay must be alike."[11] This usually meant standards would be determined to suit the desires of the least capable worker, reducing everything to "the dead level of mediocrity."[12] The best workers would inevitably be discriminated against, their superior capacity to produce more and work harder being denied its rightful superior returns. Their incentive to achievement would be extinguished and idleness and poor workmanship substituted for energy and ambition. Already in 1891 it seemed clear that "the spirit of trades unionism is strangling honest endeavour, and the hard-working, fearless, thorough artisan of ten years ago is degenerating into the shiftless, lazy, half-hearted fellow who, with unconscious irony, styles himself a Knight of Labor."[13]

Another defence of the one-to-one bargaining relationship emphasized the individual's right to dispose of his labour as he saw fit. His labour power was, after all, a workingman's source of income. "To sell that labour to whomsoever he likes, wherever he likes, in such quantities as he likes, and at such rates as he likes, is a God-given privilege which it should be the duty of ... Parliament to protect. . . . Any encroachment upon this privilege . . . can only be regarded as an unwarranted interference with individual and property rights." Although paternal legislation was probably justified to protect women and children, trade unions went beyond the bounds of responsibility, fair play, and what should be the law when they tried to stop other people from exercising their freedom of contract. Men could voluntarily combine to try and obtain agreed-upon terms; it was coercion and conspiracy to combine to impose those terms on others through the closed shop.[14]

During strikes the main concern of business commentators was to make sure the rights of "free labor" were respected. It was usually seen as an elementary question of personal liberty and individual rights. No matter how deeply strikers felt the justice of their cause, these must be respected. "As to Scabs," the *Canadian Manufacturer* editorialized,

We recognize the value of unanimity in labor; we know that

without cohesion it is powerless. We understand why men making a stand for what they honestly consider to be a just demand or remonstrance, are more or less frustrated, in some cases excusably irritated, by seeing others take up the hammer or the chisel they laid down; but with all this allowed, there can be no defence, either legal or moral, in denying another man his personal liberty or rights. Society would recoil from keeping a man out of a church door if he chooses to go in. We do not hang, burn or drown men nowadays for their religious opinions. We claim freedom at the ballot box, and punish the men who obstruct it; in fact, all men are conscious of the danger involved in interfering with personal rights. It must be so recognized in all labor struggles and labor unions will never be what they can and ought to be so long as violence is done to the non-consenting.[15]

The failure of this editorial to specify what was meant by "violence" to strikebreakers was typical. There was little discussion of picketing as a strike tactic, none that was favourable. The Canadian law on picketing and intimidation was still uncertain; business journals clearly preferred an interpretation of the law that would hold picketing to be an act of illegal restraint:

There is no doubt that the surrounding of a plant by strikers is for the one purpose of preventing others from taking their places. Any other motive suggested is a trivial sham. Moreover, under the most peaceful circumstances the work of the picketers partakes of intimidation. The ostentatious approach of a number of strikers, followed by a series of impertinent questions, most certainly tends to scare off the man who is otherwise inclined to go to work. Men who picket a shop have one main object in view, to restrict the operations of the plant, to injure the business carried on therein. This is an offense against the common law.[16]

Acts of violence in industrial disputes (thought to be a direct consequence of picketing) were almost always blamed on the strikers. Strong support was given to the use of civil authority to restore law and order. "Free laborers . . . must depend upon the public authority for the maintenance of their rights," the *Monetary Times* announced, commenting on a violent railway strike in Buffalo: "A strike which aims to prevent the places of idle men being filled makes an attack on the rights of labor outside the organization. . . . Society, unless it be prepared to abandon its civilisation, is bound to resist, and for that purpose to call upon the whole public force, "if necessary." Critical as it was of the use of mercenaries in Homestead, the *Journal of Commerce* felt no such incident was likely in Canada because "in case of any unfortunate civil troubles, we have a splendidly disciplined force of citizen soldiers who could suppress any riot without shedding blood, whose very presence, and whose discipline being shared by so many engaged in our industries, assure to a trading community the quietude essential to prosperity." Business writers supported the use of soldiers whenever they were called in Canada, with the single exception of the Hereford Railway troubles, insisting on "prompt, vigorous and decisive" suppression of violence. Most of the attitudes of businessmen to disorderly industrial disputes were reflected in the *Journal of Commerce*'s comments on rioting in Valleyfield, Quebec, in 1900 which had included resistance to the militia:

> The mob seems not to have realized that its utter criminality and folly must be put down and punished. The very mild treatment of them by the soldiers, which, at the most was a few pricks of a bayonet, misled the rioters, who needed a stern lesson as to the danger of setting law and order at defiance. Had such scenes arisen in France or Germany there would have been a rifle fusillade that would have killed a score or two of the mob. In Valleyfield, those injured were the soldiers, yet there have been violent attacks upon them by some local papers, because they cleared the streets by a very gentle display of what a bayonet feels like – a sensation which will probably check any future impulse to earn another of the kind.
>
> ... The proprietors of the Valleyfield mills are capitalists to whom Canada is under deep obligations for their enterprise in establishing and maintaining a great national industry.... It will be a sorry day for Canada when those who venture their fortunes in manufacturing enterprises can be intimidated and their property and their business interests jeopardized by rioters without the miscreants receiving the due reward of their crime against law and order. The non-service of warrants issued against the ringleaders shows lamentable weakness somewhere. Is it possible that there is a district of this lawabiding Colony where the Queen's writ does not run?[17]

It was particularly the ringleaders whom businessmen thought should be punished because they were convinced that the mass of workers were sane and sensible at best, suffering merely from ignorance and irresponsibility at worst. The ordinary worker would never get in trouble were he not duped and exploited by a variety of "hotheads," "agitators," and "troublemakers." "Ce n'est pas aux ouvriers membres des unions qu'il faut faire le reproche de ce qui se passe," said *Le Moniteur du Commerce*, "ils ne sont ni meilleurs ni plus méchants que les autres membres de la société civile; mais c'est aux agitateurs qui usent et abusent du peu d'expérience de la masse ouvrière en matière de conduite d'affaires administratives, d'industrie, de commerce, de navigations, etc." In the early days unions had been controlled by the men themselves and had done much for the working class, an 1893 obituary of organized labour stated, "But when once the fair-minded men who originated the movement were ousted from its control, and their places filled by irresponsible demagogues who fattened upon strikes and consequently provoked every collision possible between masters and men, the advantages of organized labour were largely neutralized."[18]

Pointing to the professional organizers of the American Federation of Labor and some of the larger international unions, business commentators directed a steady stream of abuse at the "walking delegates," "agitators," "souffleurs," or "jawsmiths" of organized labour. They were men, "appointés on ne sait par qui,"[19] who did no work themselves, except with their jaws, but lived like parasites on the earnings of the honest worker. "The curse of the labour union to-day is the paid agent who is not earning his bread by the sweat of his brow, but who extracts a share of the workingman's hard-earned wages to enable himself to live sumptuously and get the workingman into trouble." They had a pecuniary interest in getting the workingman into trouble because fomenting discord and strikes was the basis of their livelihood and power. Such men were "leeches," claimed the *Canadian Manufacturer*; "the vultures of the labor world," chimed in the *Journal of Commerce*, "they fatten on the carcass of those who are wounded or slain."[20]

Union organizers were usually claimed to be outsiders, particularly after 1900. They barged their way into happy factories, stirred up trouble, and undemocratically initiated unreasonable disputes. Most strikes, businessman thought, began this way: "The men at the works, who were happy and contented, have been got to join the ranks of union labor, and straightway the agitators, who live by that sort of thing, proceeded to find a grievance. . . . Only 18 per cent of the whole 2,000 men voted for this strike, be it remembered, but the majority voting at a meeting called for the purpose governs. One may feel sympathy for the uncomplaining men thus forced, through reasonless bullying, to give up earning their daily wage."[21]

A special feature of the problem of outside agitators in Canadian industrial relations was the fact that so many of the labour leaders were American. Particularly after 1902-1903 – though there had been cries of alarm at the influx of the Knights of Labor in the 1880s – the expansion of international unions into Canada set off waves of fear in the business community that Canadian industrial relations would now be controlled from a foreign country.* Anticipating later nationalist concepts of the relation of power and sovereignty, businessmen argued that "it is quite natural to assume that a society governed and controlled in the United States will have its first interests in that country."[22] Those interests might well be to protect American jobs against Canadian competition, and this could lead to wage demands being made or strikes called deliberately to cripple Canadian industries.

There were many charges that this was being done. *Le Moniteur du Commerce* thought the aim of the 1903 Montreal longshoremen's strike was "créer chez nous un vasselage au profit des ports américains," and wondered how much Gompers and company had received "par dessus l'épaule" to stir up trouble. The Royal Commission that reported in 1903 on industrial disputes in British Columbia found, against all evidence, that a sympathetic strike at Ladysmith was ultimately traceable to the intrigues of "a handful of dictators residing in the United States, and who are not in any way amenable to the laws of this country." It was "not beyond the bounds of possibility . . . that a union may be persuaded into a strike by unprincipled men for no other purpose than to cripple or destroy a Canadian industry for the benefit of its rivals." *Industrial Canada* was certain that the "real cause" of the C.P.R. strike of 1908 "could be traced back to Wall Street"; the *Journal of Commerce*, noting in 1910 the "broad fact" that "foreign dictation" was behind the Grand Trunk strike, felt it was becoming "almost a patriotic duty" to help the Canadian company against the American union's presuming dictation.[23]

The most spectacular instance of American labour "imperialism" was the United Mine Workers of America's attempt to gain control of the Nova Scotia coalfields in 1909-1910. The union's struggles to oust the P.W.A. and win bargaining rights

---

* This expansion was a product of the decision of American unions in the 1890s, particularly the A.F. of L., to send paid organizers into Canada. It represented an attempt to increase control of the continental labour market; there is no evidence that the growth of international unionism was in any way related to the growth of American investment in the Canadian economy. For further detail on American labour expansionism in this period, see R. H. Babcock, "The A.F. of L. in Canada, 1896-1908" (Ph.D. Thesis, Duke University, 1969).

at the collieries produced two of the most bitter strikes Canada had yet seen: 2500 miners were out at Glace Bay for eight months and 1700 at Springhill for twenty-one months. The Dominion Coal Company, which eventually broke both strikes (having bought out the Springhill collieries during the strike there), adopted a position of what might be called principled nationalism: "Our company will never consent to be dominated by a foreign labor union, whose interest may be allied with those of our competitors in the United States, and we will, in the interests of the preservation of our mines and property, in which the people of Nova Scotia are jointly interested with us, stand firmly in the decision."[24]

The correspondent who reported the Glace Bay strike in the *Canadian Mining Journal* rang all the changes on the theme of foreign invaders. The strike was caused by the "walking delegates" of the U.M.W.A., "men whose mouths are filled with lies," who had duped innocent workers (mostly the foreign element of the work force) to go out on strike by a "series of falsehoods," and kept them out "by falsehood invented after falsehood." Bribery, intimidation, and open lawlessness were directly traceable to the union, which had created "a virtual state of war in Cape Breton." Something had to be done to stop "the glaring lies, the naked and unashamed mendacity of the salaried American strike-breeders ... actuated solely by a desire to do damage, to run amuck." It was Canada's national policy to protect her industries from alien competition and her workers from aliens trying to steal their jobs. Yet what had happened in Nova Scotia?

> This has happened: Under the name of trades unionism every one of the protective barriers erected by our legislators against the encroachments of the United States has been swept away; a direct attack has been made upon our coal industry by alien strike leaders engaged and paid in the United States out of the funds of a United States corporation, and the result is that American coal is now being unloaded in Sydney Harbour, while some three thousand Nova Scotia miners are idling on the streets of Glace Bay and of Springhill. We have said that all this has been done in the name of trades unionism, but in reality what has happened is tantamount to sedition and to treason, which has been fomented by alien enemies who have conspired against our trade and to destroy our native institutions.[25]

These employers wanted legal protection from the American

invaders. So did the Canadian Manufacturers' Association, which enthusiastically supported bills that appeared in the Senate to outlaw foreign union agitators and adopted a general policy of encouraging "thoroughly Canadian" labour unions and labour leaders.[26] There was little or no difference between their attitude and the desires of French-Canadian business writers who called for the establishment of "unions nationales" to check the internationals in Quebec.* In isolated instances where the internationals were not more powerful and radical than Canadian unions employers were ready enough to welcome them to Canada.[27] Generally, though, as with protection their business interests and their Canadianism coincided.

Whether the outside agitators were the American brand or home-grown, the image of organized labour which emerged from this analysis was fearsome. Unions were quasi-totalitarian societies, machines run by a ruthless elite at whose word thousands of deluded followers would put down their tools and submit themselves and their families to penury and starvation for no good reason. The liberty of free and independent workers would be crushed, the rights of employers and the laws of civil society would be brushed aside, as the coarse demagogues of trade unionism made their bid to rule or ruin. "Powerful and vexatious as centralized capital may be, heartless and soulless as it has sometimes appeared," the *Financial Post* noted in 1911, "it is as nothing to the terrible power, deadly effect and blind selfishness of organized labour when working in union."[28] The *Canadian Manufacturer* supplied an apparently original parody, "The Song of the Shirk," as a theme for unionism as it understood the movement:

> With fingers that never knew toil,
>     With nose-tip swollen and red,
> A delegate sat in his easy chair,
>     Eating the laborer's bread;
> "Strike-strike-strike!
>     Nor dare return to your work!"

---

\*  "Si e'était des Canadiens qui s'aviseraient de soulever des grèves chez les Américains, ces derniers appliqueraient vite la loi Lynch. Mais non; on a si peu de fierté nationale ici, qu'on se laisse enlever d'abord des épargnes et qu'on se laisse conduire ensuite par le bout du nez par des gens de dehors.

"Et dire, hélas! que le nombre est incalculable des Canadiens-français qui se sont laissés enrégimenter dans l'Internationale et qui, par le fait même, ont perdu leur liberté, leur bien le plus précieux, et peut-être leur dignité." (*Moniteur du Commerce*, 29 mai, 1903, p. 695).

The Trade Unionist Makes War Against the Community.
*–Liberty and Progress.*

> And still with his swaggering, insolent air,
>     He sang the "Song of the Shirk."
>     . . .
>
> "Strike-strike-strike!"
>     The delegate passed this way!
> "Strike-strike-strike!"
>     He orders, you must obey!
> And ask not the reason why,
>     Nor murmur against their decree,
> For none must work when they say "No!"
>     In this country of the free!
>
> Oh! men with children dear,
>     Oh! men with daughters and wives,
> It is not the rich you are starving out,
>     But your hungry children's lives!
> Strike-strike-strike!
>     To please your masters still,
> Ye are slaves to a band of plundering knaves,
>     Who will bleed ye as long as ye will![29]

Unions naturally had to be resisted for economic reasons. In addition, and particularly in the light of the reputation unions had among businessmen, there was the challenge they offered to a man's right to run his own business. "We made up our minds that we would not interfere with labor organizations so long as they interfered simply with the men's rights," the superintendent of the Toronto Street Railway explained, "but when they interfered with the company's rights that was a different question altogether." Trade unionism was about power. It was his power, or any portion of it (for it was usually thought of in domino fashion as indivisible) that the employer refused to surrender. He might be humane and generous enough on his own terms, might make voluntary concessions to his men if they asked for them politely, but he would never have the rules and wages of his factory dictated by someone else. Nor would he negotiate when his men, by threatening to strike, "put a pistol to my head." As one of the proprietors of a Galt iron foundry told a worker in the grim strike of 1889:

> There is my factory. It is a large one, it is built of brick and stone. You might begin and take it away piecemeal – one brick at a time, one stone at a time – carrying the particles on your own shoulder over into the next county, going as slowly and deliberately as you please, and then, when all has been taken away, I

will be no nearer to yielding the management of my business to your trade union than I am now. I will never do it.[30]

The much trumpeted business "recognition" of trade unionism before World War I reduced itself to this: workingmen had a right to form an organization to *try* to bargain with employers, to *try* to shut down a firm by going on strike. But, as the *Monetary Times* summarized the new system, " recognition does not imply compliance with all or *any* demands which a union may make." Employers had equal rights to refuse any concessions, to fire workers who went out on strike, and to smash unions by bringing in strikebreakers. They also had a right, under the theory of individual freedom of contract, to ask workingmen voluntarily to contract away their right to join societies that would limit their individual rights. In a statement of employer rights which was never contradicted in business writing of the period, the *Monetary Times* defended the Toronto Street Railway Company's action in precipitating the violent 1886 strike by enforcing "ironclad" agreements with its men:

The street car drivers and conductors had voluntarily contracted away their undoubted right to combine. It was a condition of service in the company that they should not join any labor union; this condition they had formally accepted by signing a written engagement to that effect. The condition was one which, under the freedom of contract, the company had a right to make; those who did not like it had the right to prefer connection with a labor union to service under the company. That was the alternative, and it coerced no man's action, but left every one to his own free choice. But when the men accepted this condition, it was a breach of contract to join a labor union; and they cannot complain if the penalty of dismissal was enforced.[31]

In the extreme this position led to an absolute unwillingness to have anything whatever to do with unions. It was best expressed by a former premier of British Columbia and multi-millionaire coal and timber magnate, James Dunsmuir, to a Royal Commission trying to find out why labour relations had gone sour in his province. Although the Vancouver *World* felt he was "not an extremist in his views," Dunsmuir came as close as Canadian business ever did to echoing Vanderbilt's "The public be damned":

Q. Do you know of any real cause for the difficulty which the men have now in these mines?

A. No, I do not. The only trouble is because I won't let them belong to the union. They can belong to the union if they like – I don't care. I have my rights. I can hire them if I like, and they can work if they like. . . .

Q. You have no other motive for refusing to recognize except – ?

A. Except, that I want the management of my own works, and if I recognize the union, I cannot have that. Then we are dictated to by a committee of the union as to what should be done and what should not be done. . . .

Q. Have you not, when you became aware of a man belonging to the union, got rid of him?

A. You mean fired the heads of the union?

Q. Yes?

A. Every time.

Q. And have you done that in pursuance of a settled policy of antagonism to organization?

A. Yes, around the works.

Q. You recognize, surely, the right of the workingmen to organize?

A. Of course, that is their own right. They can organize and belong to whatever union they like.

Q. Just on the same principle that you consider you have an absolute right to handle your own property?

A. Yes, I think that is my right; they have their rights.

Q. You hold that you have an absolute right to deal with your own property?

A. Just as I like.

Q. Did it ever occur to you that wealth carried some corresponding obligations with it – the possession of large riches and lands?

A. No sir. From my standpoint it doesn't. . . .

Q. You don't recognize any third party to the social contract; it is simply you and your men?

A. Yes.[32]

This kind of ignorance only fertilized the union movement. Labour's best friends could not have invented a better stereotype of the reactionary employer than the real James Dunsmuir.* As anyone could see, the days of his kind of imperial arrogance were num-

---

* Nor could the strongest believer in the corrupting effect of great wealth have invented a more perfect example of drunken, perverted dissipation than that supplied by the Dunsmuir offspring. See the extraordinary account of the family fortunes, told by one of the descendants, in James F. Audain, *From Coal Mine to Castle* (New York, 1955).

bered. If employers were to maintain the freedom of action and the authority that almost all of them believed unionism threatened, if they were to prevent the industrial violence endemic in the United States from spilling into Canada, some positive alternative would have to be found to end the hostility developing between capital and labour. Something would have to be done to maintain or restore the common "interest" the two great factors of production were supposed to have, to create the ideal situation where the worker's attitude to his bosses would be to "throw his hat up in the air and cheer for their success, for their success is his success."[33]

One solution to industrial conflict that was often seen as a panacea was the idea of profit-sharing. Widely discussed in North America in the late nineteenth and early twentieth centuries and among the topics investigated by the Royal Labor Commission, schemes for profit-sharing were frequently considered in Canadian trade journals from the 1880s through the Laurier years. Profit-sharing seemed an obvious and easy way of re-uniting the interests of employer and employed, of creating a new "industrial partnership" or "democracy in business" in which every man in an organization would have an incentive to work for its success. Its general adoption, claimed the *Canadian Manufacturer,* "would introduce a millenium where strikes, lock-outs, labor disputes and unpleasant relations between employer and employee would be known no more."[34] Although comment on the idea was often sympathetic, there are only scattered examples of Canadian businessmen introducing explicit profit-sharing plans: the Dodge Stove Works in Oshawa in the early 1880s; T. S. Simms & Co., brush manufacturers in the Maritimes in the early 1890s; the H. W. Petrie machinery firm of Toronto and the British Columbia Electric Railway Company in the early 1900s. It is not clear why there were so few attempts at profit-sharing. Businessmen sometimes objected to any plan in which losses would not also be shared and probably accurately judged that workers would not accept that kind of "equitable" profit-sharing arrangement.[35] More generally, systematic profit-sharing would be a radical innovation, difficult to administer, and possibly ineffective. Many firms, however, particularly those employing white-collar workers, met their employees' interest in incentives half-way with annual bonuses geared to profits.

Profit-sharing was a formalized version of straightforward employer generosity. This, businessmen always thought, whether they practised it or not, was the most effective way to avoid having to negotiate with a trade union. The employer paternalism and more formalized industrial welfare and technical education movements discussed in Chapter 3 were all recognized as having anti-union implications. One 1882 account of a firm party in the *Canadian Manufacturer* was entitled, "Employers and Employed. How to Avoid Trouble Between Them and Prevent Strikes." A clinching argument for welfare work in factories was to see it "as the surest safeguard against the more aggressive and most objectionable demands of socialists and labor agitators."[36] Perhaps technical education, by instilling skill, motivation, and an appreciation of workmanship in the men, would unfit them as candidates for trade unionism. On the other hand the need for labour's support in the struggle to establish technical education meant that the C.M.A. had to be careful that technical education institutions did not become "scab hatcheries,"[37] and on the whole the anti-union implications of paternalism and other schemes to benefit workers were not emphasized in the business press.

Still, they lurked in the background, and occasionally the velvet glove was taken off when workers were ungrateful for employer generosity. In 1908 and 1910 respectively the C.P.R. and Grand Trunk cut off the pension rights of strikers who did not return to their jobs on command. Both systems' pension plans had clauses withdrawing the benefits accruing to workers "voluntarily leaving the employment of the company when their services are in demand."[38] The Grand Trunk, in particular, refused to make any concessions at all, and for years after the 1910 strike fought the federal government's efforts to have the pensions restored. It seemed to be a matter of principle: if the pensions were rewards for faithful service they should not be given to men who had proven unfaithful. A writer in the *Financial Post* explained exactly why the railways behaved as they did in strikes:

Although a great corporation of this kind is under a certain moral obligation to provide for the declining years of the men who have worn out their lives in its service, as yet in America there is no legal obligation upon them to do so. The funds which they have provided they regard as something special. Instead of taking the pensions as the laborers' right they take them as a special means of rewarding long and faithful service, which of course being nullified by a strike, is thus looked upon as a means of preventing them. As they are thus designed in part as a preventative of strikes it is necessary when a strike occurs that those who cease work voluntarily shall be deprived of their interest in the fund. If that policy were not rigorously followed the pension funds would be absolutely valueless as strike preventatives. . . . The many cases of individual hardship suffered in this way . . . though most regrettable in themselves, may yet have a good effect in moderating the attitude of the railway unions in future controversies.[39]

This was the limitation of both the older paternalism and the newer welfare work. As the *Journal of Commerce* put it in 1890, benefits were concessions from the "strong and wise" to the "ignorant and weak,"[40] premised on the latter's perpetual acceptance of that condition. What the left hand gave to faithful servants the right hand could take away from ungrateful troublemakers. There was no redistribution of power, but changing the existing power relationship in industry was what trade unionism was about. Paternalist methods did work when used by shrewd and progressive employers[41] (and would be given new sophistication and popularity after World War I with the development of company union plans, many based on Mackenzie King's Colorado Plan.) But they were not and could not be a complete alternative to the challenge organized labour was presenting.

Assuming that worker organization was a fact of life, was there any way of learning to live with unions, instead of engaging in life-and-death struggles when the men went out on strike? Businessmen saw no easy substitute for the strike as a method of resolving industrial disputes. Compulsory arbitration, a favourite proposal of concerned outsiders, was thought to raise far more problems than it could solve: it would encourage unions to escalate demands in the hope that arbitrators would split the difference, add the already untrustworthy force of public opinion to industrial disputes, and ultimately involve governments in attempts at wage-fixing on one hand and coercion of disputants on the other.[42] No one objected in theory to submitting disputes to non-binding arbitration and conciliation procedures, and occasionally businessmen successfully arbitrated local disputes and called for formalization of such procedures.[43]

One way of forcing a measure of responsibility on organized labour was to have unions made responsible for the consequences of their acts through legal incorporation. This was thought of as a way of equalizing a situation in which one party to contracts and disputes was responsible at law and the other was not, a situation that seemed to give unions the special privilege of being beyond the law. Interest in having Canadian unions made legally responsible was greatly stimulated by the 1901 Taff Vale decision in England holding unions responsible for strikers' actions. The C.M.A. resolved in favour of incorporation of trade unions and contributed $9000 to the prosecution of what was hoped would be a test case to determine Canadian law on the same issue.[44] When the Metallic Roofing Company seemed to have succeeded in its damage suit against the Amalgamated Metal Workers' Association, *Industrial Canada* explained to its readers what it took to be the consequences of the precedent:

> These industrial highwaymen have learned the lesson that they can no longer hold their employers up at pistol point and order them to stand and deliver without themselves being called upon to suffer the consequences provided by the law in such cases. Possibly the irresponsible stripling who has nothing which can be seized to satisfy a claim, or the well-fed delegate who can watch the trouble from a safe distance, may still be anxious to continue under a career of lawless extravagance, but the time has come when the sober mechanic, who has a home with a wife and little ones to provide for, is going to have a say in the management of union affairs. He is the one who must ultimately pay the price of the union's folly, and he is the one to whom the employers may now look for assistance in restoring industrial peace and harmony.[45]

But the case dragged on inconclusively, the C.M.A. resolved to avoid all future involvement in legal fights, the law was still confused, and in the 1970s unions were still resisting proposals to have them incorporated.

A more ominous theme of comment on the labour situation stressed the need for counter-organization by employers. Beginning in the 1880s there was a current of business muttering to the effect that the organization of labour had upset the balance in the industrial system and it was necessary for business to use the same methods to create countervailing power. "When bad men conspire, good men must combine," ran the old saying.[46] Observing events in the United States, Frederic Nicholls of the C.M.A. thought he could discern how historians of the future would interpret the rise of collectivism in industry:

> The historian should now be accumulating data which will enable him to write in the not distant future a history of "strikes" and "trusts" as they now prevail and affect social and political life in the American Republic. And in so writing he will necessarily show that strikes, and its [sic] equally objectionable corollary, the boycott, were the direct cause of those other objectionable things – trusts and combines. . . .

The historian will show that organized labor was the aggressor, and that it first brought the influence of the strike to bear in enforcing its demands; that it soon called the boycott into existence as its auxiliary; and that these weapons proved to be of such terrible and potential character as to cause it to forget that while it was well to possess the strength of a giant, it was cowardly to use that strength indiscriminately . . . he will also remind his readers, on the authority of Holy Writ, that he who taketh the sword is liable to perish by the keen thrusts of that warlike weapon. He will also suggest that strikes and boycotts are a species of boomerang that inevitably return to smite and injure those who hurl them; and that while these boomerangs go out in the form of strikes and boycotts, they return bearing marked resemblance to trusts and combinations.[47]

This ridiculous distortion did reflect a real process, the coming together of employers in combinations jointly to suppress unions. Although the occasional continental business association was formed to deal with international unions, such as the National Founders' Association and National Metal Trades' Association, employer organization in Canada usually took place on a local basis, all employers in a specific trade in a city or locality combining for concerted anti-union action. By 1903 in Vancouver, for example, there were associations of shipowners, retail merchants, publishers, shingle manufacturers, lumber manufacturers, contractors, box manufacturers, master plasterers, and master plumbers, and in that year a city-wide organization was formed to refuse to hire any workers on strike for a closed shop at the Vancouver Engineering Works.[48]

The only enduring general anti-union organization seems to have been the Toronto Employers' Association, founded in 1902 and surviving at least until 1911. Led by radical anti-union manufacturers, and modelled on American employers' associations, the T.E.A. proposed to give financial assistance to employers suffering from strikes and to "such workmen as remain faithful to the employer," arbitrate as many disputes as it could, conduct its own labour exchange for independent workingmen, blacklist labour troublemakers, draw up uniform codes of apprenticeship and factory rules, and sponsor legal actions against unions and government bodies toadying to them. In its early years the T.E.A. apparently succeeded in maintaining and expanding the open-shop principle in Toronto.[49] There had been some talk in 1901-1902 of founding a national employers' association, but the C.M.A. made an explicit decision not to follow its American counterpart, the National Association of Manufacturers, into overt anti-union activities, and refused to organize or give funds for employers' associations.[50]

Still, it is clear from surviving trade association minutes that concerted anti-union activity on a municipal level was very extensive, probably normal, in Canada.[51] Such activities were held to be legal, including the right of associations to sue members who had violated an agreement to form a common anti-labour front. In at least two cases judges agreed that if workers had a right to organize against their employers, the reciprocal right also existed.[52] Forming power blocks to resist organized labour was not much of an alternative, but employers wondered what else they could do.

Chapter 5

# Business, Protection, and Nationalism

What is the creed and the calling that we of the North
uphold –
It is never the cry for power, it is never the greed of
gold,
Let the east and south and west contend like wolves for
a maverick's bone,
But Canada for the Canadians is the creed that we
call our own

We don't need the marts of Europe, nor the trade of
the Eastern isles,
We don't need the Yankee's corn and wine, nor the
Asiatic's smiles.
For what so good as our home-made cloth and under
the wide blue dome,
Will you tell me where you have tasted bread like
the bread that is baked at home?

– from "Made in Canada," by Pauline Johnson,
composed for the Canadian Manufacturers'
Association, 1903

The protective tariff, or, as it was originally called, the National Policy, was the most important issue in Canadian business and political life in the late nineteenth and early twentieth centuries. The maintenance of the National Policy with only minor alterations through eight general elections, particularly those of 1891 and 1911, was the most impressive demonstration of political influence by a group in the business community during the period. On no other issue did businessmen present such elaborate and persistent and successful justifications of their position. On no other issue did they so completely and successfully manage to identify their own interests with those of the Canadian nation. Their interests, of course, were in limiting the freedom of foreign producers to compete openly in the Canadian market.

Manufacturers were, naturally, the strongest advocates of tariff protection. The main aim of their association and its journals was to maintain and extend the National Policy. There were lingering pockets of free-trade sentiment among a few dissident manufacturers, some importers, and Western merchants allied with the agrarian community. On the whole, though, their opposition to the tariff was seldom vocal. Of the major business papers only the Winnipeg *Commercial* and the *Monetary Times* were cool towards the National Policy. The former journal was editorially insignificant after about 1902 and the latter changed its position in the early 1900s, becoming rabidly protectionist by 1911. Business comment on the trade question was overwhelmingly weighted in favour of protection, so much so that there was no real debate among businessmen on the question. The National Policy was national business policy.

One common way in which businessmen tried to phrase the issue was to deny the terms of the debate and ignore the economists by dismissing all opposition to the tariff as useless theorizing. Businessmen loved to think of themselves as practical men; as such they knew that the practical requirements of the country demanded protection. As president of the C.M.A. in 1896, A. E. Kemp warned against those "men of respectability and influence in public life in Canada who never tire of propounding theories on these questions, whose practical business experience is limited, and whose ideas have become crystallized through research in reference to the questions in other countries, whose conditions are altogether different from ours." He had in mind critics of the tariff like Professor Adam Shortt whose position was dismissed in 1905 by the *Journal of Commerce* as no more than "theorising gone mad" and "a fallacy that has been exposed so often that it no longer deceives any but theorists who live secluded from the business world." The tactics of captains of industry could only be criticized by other captains of industry. But of course most practical Canadian businessmen knew their business requirements from experience. "In principle I am an ardent Free Trader," a British Columbia lumberman wrote to Finance Minister Fielding. "Yet we must admit it is not always easy to make our pet theories square with existing conditions," he added, asking for more protection from his American competitors.[1]

Another way of stressing the "practical" nature of the tariff debate was to emphasize the practical consequences of dismantling the National Policy. In 1880 Edward Gurney, president of the Ontario Manufacturers' Association, had predicted that within twelve months no political leader would dare resist the National Policy, instituted only the previous year: "so many new interests will have been created and so much capital invested in manufactures, that their very existence will be at issue 'and modify considerably any argument in favour of a return to the old revenue tariff. The 'vested interest' principle will then enter into the question and will be of such magnitude as to demand and obtain recognition." To a large extent this is what happened. By the end of the 1880s hundreds of manufacturers and tens of thousands of workers depended on the tariff. The theoretical merits of the issue aside, the economic consequence of a return to the old system would be a major, if short-term, disruption of the Canadian economy. The political consequences of that were frightening. In his maiden speech to the Senate in 1897, financier George Cox was saying in effect that vested interests had overpowered the Liberal Party's free-trade principles:

> We have created industries upon the basis of protection, industries in which many millions of dollars of private capital have been invested, and upon the credit of which many millions more of working capital have been borrowed from our banking institutions. It is not necessary now to discuss the merits or demerits of the system under which these industries have been created, the fact remains that they do exist, that large investments have been made, large liabilities incurred, and that legislation tending to embarrass important interests would be disastrous.[2]

When free traders insisted on debating the issue anyway, protectionists replied with a wide variety of positive justifications of the tariff. Some were variations of the defences of combines discussed in Chapter 2. More a demand than an argument, for example, was the cry for fair treatment. Surely it was very unfair to deny a person who had invested his capital in a protected industry the right to a decent return. All the Beethoven Piano Company wanted from the tariff, it told Customs Minister Paterson, was to be in a position "to make something out of our business." The Markham Woollen Mills wanted the duty changed solely so that it could earn a "living profit" on its investment.[3] In most cases, of course, manufacturers said they were only asking for protection against the unfair competitive practices of foreigners who, they charged, dumped and slaughtered their goods on Canadian markets at least as often as they tried to sell them at fair prices. Complementary arguments attacked the quality of foreign-made products and the unreasoning prejudice of

97

Canadian consumers against Canadian products. The tariff was only necessary to force consumers to make a fair and rational choice: "there is no doubt that all our manufacturers require is a fair field and no favor and that purchasers would be willing to judge articles on their merits without giving a preference to an imported article merely because it is imported."[4]

More sophisticated public defences of the tariff rested heavily on demonstrations that protection was also in the interests of other and larger groups in the community. It was easy, for instance, to defend the tariff in terms of the jobs and wages it created or protected. Every new factory established under the National Policy seemed to add that many more jobs to the country. Every threat to the National Policy was a threat to the jobs it sustained. Whenever a plant was hard-pressed to meet foreign competition its owners could remind the government of the number of employees (and voters) whose jobs were at stake. "Gentlemen, I vote for the National Policy that . . . gave work to those that wanted work," argued an imaginary workman in an 1887 Industrial League pamphlet, "I don't see how any working-man can do anything else when he thinks of the suffering of the unemployed."[5] It was, perhaps, free-trade orthodoxy in the late nineteenth century that governments were not responsible for making jobs for people; but it was certainly not protectionist orthodoxy. The difference between the two attitudes was that between "gruff, surly, unfeeling Free Trade," and "kindly, sympathetic, labor-helping Protection."[6]

The tariff was also presented to labour as the only way to keep Canadian wages above the semi-starvation rates existing in other countries, even England itself. "It is imperative that factory workers on this side of the Atlantic should be kept in mind of the shamefully low wages paid to their fellow-workers in the Old World," noted the *Canadian Manufacturer,* "so that they may be able to see what Free Trade would do for them if we had it." It and the other protectionist journals proceeded to do just that,* as did businessmen petitioning the government for more pro-

---

* "One person in every seven in England is in a stage of pauperism. We have only to look at the immigrants who land on our wharves to see that Canada has no class of her population in such poverty as these people display. Look at the millions of children attending the schools of this country, amongst whom a ragged or starved child could not be found. In England millions of children are in rags, millions too are ill-fed. Between free-trade with a vast army of paupers, a myriad of ragged, hungry children as in England, and protection without workhouses, or poor relief, or a pauper class, or hordes of hunger bitten children, the people of Canada have made their choice – they think much of the overwhelming facts that prove the benefits of a protective tariff; and they

tection. "Our Manager thought it was really pitiable and degrading to see [English] women in short skirts, clogs for shoes, with horrible dirty faces and hands doing the work which we are accustomed to seeing men do," the Merchants' Cotton Company informed the Finance Minister in 1902. "If we are not to get the duty . . . there is nothing for it but sooner or later we must reduce our wages to correspond with what is being paid in England." In this reasoning protection was no longer a subsidy to a small group of businessmen. It was, as *Industrial Canada* argued in 1911, "not primarily the protection of the individual manufacturers or of the manufacturing class; it is the protection of the workman, the great class of employees, the men and women who have to live on what they can make from week to week."[7]

It was much more difficult to justify the tariff to an agricultural community for whom it offered little beyond a higher cost of living. Of course manufacturers always offered to support the extension of high tariffs to all agricultural "manufacturers,"[8] and probably always received the support of significant agricultural groups to whom preserving and expanding the home market was important. Arguments for enlarging home markets through promoting urban growth seemed to coincide well with the transition to mixed farming in central Canada in the 1880s and 1890s. In these years perhaps there was something to the manufacturers' argument that "the farmer can be benefitted more by the trade between the tail gate of his waggon and the kitchen pantry of the employés of the factories and workshops in his nearest market town than he can possibly be in the freight carried back and forth across the ocean."[9] But as the wheat economy boomed through the first decade of the century it was patently ridiculous of protectionists to argue that thriving Canadian urban centres would be necessary to prevent a glut of farm products on the world markets which would reduce Canadian farmers to little better than Chinese or Indian peasants.[10] As the great tariff fight of 1911 drew near, protectionists concentrated on defending the tariff as the East's just reward for the (also just) subsidies it had given agriculture in general and the West in particular, as well as taking the last refuge of appealing to the patriotism of farmers.

Protectionists had little patience with anyone who tried to argue that it was no business of government to subsidize economic interest groups. Activist government was so obviously an integral part of protectionist theory that the question was hardly

---

regard the stale, doctrinaire, exploded theories of free trade as among the curiosities of literature." (*Journal of Commerce,* March 8, 1892, p. 492.)

worth discussing. When it was raised momentarily in 1892 the *Canadian Manufacturer* took its political theory from St. Paul's text, "he that provideth not for his own household denieth the faith and is worse than an infidel," and ennobled the National Policy with the mandate of Heaven: "The nation is but an enlarged household, and those who have it in charge, that is, the Government, are under a divine injunction to protect its people." When the *Globe* persisted in chastising industry for relying on government, the journal denied there was anything unsound or unreasonable about such a situation:

> Protection in some form or another has existed in human society beyond a time when history became a recorder of facts. It is to be seen everywhere and in every sentient thing, and it is nowhere more forcibly and emphatically expressed than by the mother when she shields her child from any impending or apparent danger. . . . It is the duty of the parental government to protect the home brood against the encroachments of the intruder. It is the duty of the law to protect the just against the outrages of the wicked. It is the duty of those who bear the flag – who represent the power and glory of the Empire—to protect those who may be entitled to its protection. It is equally the duty of government to protect the industries of the people of the country against the encroachment of the people of any other country.[11]

Despite the familial imagery of these arguments, protectionists in the business community were too canny to follow the more theoretical writers, who seem to have dominated the earlier discussion, into stressing the infant industries argument.[12] Most of them knew too well that the infancy of many Canadian industries would be long indeed. Protection was to be a permanent condition. Thus the *Canadian Manufacturer* indignantly denied that the manufacturers who originated the National Policy had ever promised to be as efficient as foreign industries after a few years. Such an idea, it said, was "excessively ridiculous." For much the same reason protectionists thought bounties were poor substitutes for tariffs, and gave little shrift to attempts to obscure the principles of the National Policy with talk of "incidental" protection or reciprocity of tariffs with the United States.[13]

The equation of the tariff with Canadian nationalism does not seem to have been a feature of the earliest protectionist movements,[14] or for that matter the earliest nationalist movements, but began in the depression of the 1870s and mounted steadily towards a climax in the Canadian Manufacturers' Association's

*—Protectionists welcomed the branch-plant
creating effects of the tariff.*

Sir Wilfrid: "Why should I lower it
when I am getting such results as this?"

tariff campaign of 1902-1905 and the election of 1911. Nor, at first, did the nationalism of the manufacturers' National Policy involve visions of an east-west transcontinental economy. Few of the business contemporaries of John A. Macdonald and the protectionist politicians seem to have grasped the connection between the National Policy and the government's other national policies. Until markets in the West actually started to appear in the early 1900s they were more interested in the possibilities of foreign markets and government encouragement of Canadian exports.[15] Only in the twentieth century, following almost exactly upon a C.M.A. excursion to Western Canada in 1903, did east-west, sea-to-sea arguments begin to appear as reinforcements of the National Policy.[16] The nationalism businessmen equated with the tariff preceded and was largely independent of any major concern with Western expansion.

Unemployment in Canada had a peculiar implication for national survival in that unemployed Canadians could and did leave for the United States. In an age when population growth was thought to be a vital index of national success, emigration was a basic sign of national failure. Therefore the job-creating effects of the National Policy were more than a measure of unemployment relief. They strengthened the nation itself by keeping Canadians north of the border. Instancing urban growth as proof that the tariff inhibited rather than stimulated the exodus to the United States, protectionists never let free traders forget that the alternative to the National Policy would be depopulation of the country as workingmen followed industrial job opportunities to the United States. And, as *Industrial Canada* reminded the I.O.D.E., "most of the young Canadians who leave Canada to become citizens of the United States are almost as completely lost to the Empire as if they were killed on the field of battle." Therefore, the man who bought Canadian products and thus kept Canadian workers at home was a "practical loyalist."[17]

But the nationalist appeal of the National Policy was more complex, more deeply rooted than a straightforward concern for keeping workingmen in the country.* It rested on a view of the

---

\* By not realizing this in my article, "Canadianizing American business: the roots of the branch plant," in Ian Lumsden, ed., *Close the 49th Parallel, Etc.: The Americanization of Canada* (Toronto: 1970), pp. 27-42, I may have given a misleadingly exaggerated impression of the importance of concern for jobs. In Ontario, the stronghold of protectionism, the exodus was least a problem, but that was where most of the branch-plants that caused so much comment located. In Quebec, where concern for emigration was strongest, the possibilities of developing labour-intensive industry, either through domestic

kind of society that constituted a nation, a view of the process of economic development that was necessary, indeed ordained, if Canada were to become a nation in the full sense of the word. By equating industrial development with national development it established an image of the manufacturer as nation-builder and bound together his interests and the interests of the Dominion.

At first glance the standard argument that a country ought to have a diversity of industries seems based on the idea of a society's duty to provide jobs for its people. But it rested on a more basic assumption, one which nicely countered the free trader's emphasis on the mobility and adaptability of labour. In their discussions of labour, protectionists emphasized the "varying tastes and capacities" of workingmen,[18] and insisted that the national economy be adjusted to the diverse needs of the people rather than ·vice versa. Each worker had peculiar abilities. A society that did not utilize all the talents of its people was not making the most effective use of its human resources. As Macdonald had said in 1878, "we must develop the minds of the people and their energies . . . develop the skill and genius with which God has gifted them." As George E. Drummond echoed him a quarter-century later speaking to the C.M.A., "Diversified employment will develop our people, . . . to utilize all the powers of body and mind in a nation you must have something that suits everybody." Thus, even if Canada had jobs for all its people in one industry, the nation would have failed in its duty to develop their varied abilities to the fullest. This is a major reason why protectionists were fond of arguing that no purely agricultural country had ever become great, that the most desirable qualities of civilized life could never develop in a community consisting, as "Mr. Hooley" put it, solely of "chewers of wood an' dhrinkers of wather."[19]

These notions were linked to the belief that economic progress or development was a straight line growth from lower through higher stages of manufacture. If wealth was created primarily by labour, by working on raw materials, then the more labour that was added in the manufacturing process the more wealth would be created for the community. "Every hour of labour that is put on an article adds that much to the nation's wealth." To buy goods from other countries meant paying for foreign labour

investment or the creation of branch-plants, were not as great for a number of economic reasons. Hence the heavy reliance, even by business papers, on colonization as the alternative to emigration. Neither *Le Prix Courant* nor *Le Moniteur du Commerce*, though protectionist, ever had much to say about the National Policy and emigration.

rather than Canadian labour; alternatively, to sell goods abroad to which the maximum value had not been added through final processing meant wasting opportunities for creating wealth, or, in another image, "pumping the life blood out of our country and sending it to vitalize the artisans and laborers of another country." Another Montreal Drummond explained this neo-mercantilist argument in some detail:

If we are to advance in wealth and population, if we are to build a nation, we must be able to offer fair work and fair wages, and to do this we must develop our natural resources, more especially in those directions that require the greatest amount of labor. When we have labor and the producing power of the earth working together, whether in agriculture, mining, or the utilizing of our forests, we are doing this, and the highest point to which we can bring the earth's product, with the consequent increase of value through extra labor expended within our own boundaries, the better for our country. So, I reason, that if instead of shipping our forest products in practically a raw state, we can carry the process of finishing to a higher stage, then our forests will of necessity yield to us so much greater benefit. To a very large extent the value of a forest tree is the value received for the labor expended in hewing it into square timber, sawing it into boards or turning it into an article of furniture, and it stands to reason that the tree that was by Canadian labor transformed into furniture, has yielded more than its fellow that was exported in the form of square timber, or that a spruce tree shipped in the form of paper yields more than if it had left Canada in the form of sawn logs or even pulp.[20]

Canada was richly endowed with resources of all kinds. Resources were provided by nature in an undeveloped state for man to process by applying his own labour power. Therefore it was the Divine or natural intention that Canadians should develop a complete industrial civilization. If nature had endowed the whole Dominion from the Atlantic to the Pacific with one vast stretch of fertile land, no minerals, timber, or waterfalls, *Industrial Canada* argued, there might be some ground for believing that Canada was naturally an exclusively agricultural country. "But nature has endowed Canada not only with rich agricultural land, but with timber, iron, copper, lead, and with all the economic minerals . . . . A country so wonderfully endowed with varied resources was surely intended by nature to be populated by a nation of varied occupations. It was intended that the raw materials so abundantly provided should be worked up into finished products by a manufacturing population . . . ." If Canadians failed to realize their industrial possibilities, then, they would be betraying the mandate of nature, the injunction to man to enrich the earth by applying labour to unprocessed materials. "Blessed as we are with so many natural resources, we would be false to ourselves and to our country if we did not encourage their use and development," read the C.M.A.'s memorial to the Tariff Commission in 1906. If Canadians were satisfied to see their raw resources shipped off to other countries, *Industrial Canada* argued the next year, "then we are not worthy of the magnificent resources with which nature has endowed us."[21]

The rising concern for conservation in the later years of the Laurier regime was also used by protectionists to reinforce their position. In a number of statements apparently supporting conservation, protectionist businessmen redefined it to mean the preservation of wealth within the boundaries of Canada and/or the fullest utilization of natural resources through domestic processing. It was "reckless squandering of these resources" to hand them over to other countries to be manufactured, claimed one writer. "True national economy," argued another, was "that a people shall take its raw material and bring it to the highest point of perfection possible." The point was not to keep resources out of everyone's hands (and therefore render them useless) by locking them up; but rather to keep the resources out of foreign hands while doing everything possible to realize their wealth for Canadians.[22]

When the equation of home manufacturing with national development and fulfillment was supplemented by primitive notions that trading with a nation meant dependence on it and that all importing was a drain on national wealth, protectionists had constructed a powerful buttress to their more practical role as providers of jobs, cash, and markets. They soon gained support for a more aggressive resource development policy than tariffs, the attempt to apply the "manufacturing condition" to the processing of raw materials. As described by economic historians such as Main, Aitken, and especially Nelles, the export duties, prohibitions, and regulations applied to commodities ranging from saw-logs to nickel were a policy of "insistence" that Canadian employment and national wealth be increased by processing primary goods within the country. The manufacturing condition was the other side of the tariff coin.[23]

If manufacturers were the leaders in resource development, which was critical for national development, it was clear that their interest was inseparable from the national interest. Accordingly, there was J. J. Cassidey at the 1895 C.M.A. meeting telling "the glorious array of patriots" present, "No other body of men better comprehends the true interests of Canada – no other body is more concerned in her prosperity"; and R. W. Elliott proclaiming to the world, "the recommendations of this association have never been dictated by motives of selfish gain to any individual or any one class of industries . . . but by a broad view of the interests of the Canadian people in every part of the Dominion." There was Charles B. Waterous telling his fellow manufacturers in 1903, "The growth and success of our industrial interests means the advancement of Canada, conversely anything that retards or hampers this growth, must be against the best interests of our country." And George E. Drummond hinting to the 1903 convention, "that when we go to our legislators we will find they are just as good Canadians as ourselves."[24] And there were many others. After all, the manufacturers were the men in the vanguard of Canadian national progress and prosperity.

Standing as they did on the hallowed ground of patriotism, protectionists could demand support solely because of their Canadianism. The National Policy – the tariff – was the keystone of all national policies. The home market was the "natural heritage" of the Canadian manufacturer.[25] Buying "Made in Canada" products was the consumer's patriotic duty, an integral part of national loyalty. Even when it meant a little financial sacrifice, a little setting aside of selfishness, this was no more than Canadians should do when the future of their country was at stake. "We cannot afford, for what seems personal profit, to pull down the national structure we have spent so much to build," B. E. Walker reminded his countrymen when he thought the nation was at stake in 1911. "If there are any who seek only their own gain and who do not care whether Canada is built rightly or not, they deserve little consideration on our part." The manufacturers were asking the farmer that year just to pay a little price for being Canadian:

There are things which rise above the level of mercenary values. There are things which cannot be measured in dollars and cents. Such a thing is our national destiny. We must not gamble with our future in the hope of winning some momentary gain. Even though it were assured that the grain growers of the West would add to their profits, even though it were shown that from the standpoint of dollars and cents the advantages would offset the disadvantages, yet with the prospect of a loss of our national individuality at the end of the road, the way must be shunned.[26]

The fact that National Policy men waved the old flag mightily in the 1891 and 1911 elections and often enough in between did not mean they had any significant interest in the imperialist implications of Canada's continued autonomy from the United States. The imperialist alternative, tighter imperial commercial relations, would have defeated the purpose of protectionism which was to reduce competition regardless of the nationality of the competitor. "What difference would it make to a man if he were kicked to death by a mule or by a jackass?" asked the *Canadian Manufacturer* in 1894, apropos of imperial preferences. Canadians would prefer to expand their trade with Britain, but only by increasing the duties against the rest of the world, not by reducing the protection offered Canadian manufacturers. Protectionists grudgingly accepted the unilateral preferential tariffs instituted in 1897 as better than the disastrous effects of either reciprocity or a general demolition of the National Policy; but in an 1898 resolution the C.M.A. made it clear that the minimum rates had to be "high enough to protect existing Canadian industries from the competition of countries having lower priced labor, cheaper raw materials and capital, and whose long established industries give them great advantages over those of Canada." If and when the minimal tariffs were too low to protect Canadian industries, manufacturers lobbied energetically against a policy which seemed to be "sacrificing on the altar of Imperial sentiment the industries which are the bulwark of Canada."[27] The Empire, yes, but Canada first was their decided policy. As such, protectionist sentiment in Canada worked to frustrate movements for a more meaningful economic imperialism.

Protectionism also tended to alter the Canadian climate of opinion about things British because of the interest its defenders had in demonstrating the bad effects of free trade on the mother country. In a 1911 C.M.A. Executive Council meeting a member complained about the trend of the government's policy being to belittle protection with references to the prosperity of England. "He felt that we should take them at their word and show to the people of Canada just what the conditions were in free-trade England. He felt that if the unemployment and poverty there prevailing could be realistically portrayed the theoretical support of free-trade would tumble to the ground." Protectionists had been trying to portray these conditions for years, doing all they could to encourage a Canadian image of Britain as economically stagnant, poverty-stricken, riddled with class divisions, and suffering from unprogressive leadership. This is the image of Britain protectionism spread in Canada:

> Huge mounds of black and dirty-white rubbish, melancholy asses cropping the sparse, shrivelled herbage on the banks of the worked out pits; stagnant pools, spreading like dead seas between the jumbled, natural and artificial hills; cinder-strewn

meadows threaded by filthy footpaths ending at smutting stiles; high roads fringed with a dreary continuity of dingy red brick houses in the midst of which a yellow washed house looks almost as pure as a lily; small boys clustered on the roads, kicking and punching and bespattering their feminine acquaintances; bigger ones loafing around the little dingy public houses; narrow ragged-hedged lanes, leading nowither in particular, pitfalled with inky puddles through which unwashed, unshaven, heavy-booted men flounder and splash, with their hands in their coat-pockets and vicious looking dogs cowering at their heels; jaundiced canals crowded with lanky, black barges; sloping tramways, almost obliterated by gritty, viscious black mud; crossing and converging railways with roadside stations that look like recently emptied soot-warehouses, gibbeted black colliery wheels, dilapidated engine houses and cottages sinking, on one side, into the undermined earth; dingy red and clay colored cones and domes; iron works' furnaces, chimneys of all kinds, sending up smoke and flames. This is no exaggeration picture of what I saw.[28]

These and similar pictures of English life were not apt to increase Canadians' urge to strengthen cultural and economic relations with free-trade Britain.

If the United States was a violent country racked with class struggle and industrial warfare, it was nevertheless a North American nation that had shown what protection could achieve. It was, after all, the wealthiest country in the world, whose progress in the nineteenth century had been astounding. Its history of industrial development under protection would "stand before the whole world as a monument to business foresight and brains in government." Canada should profit by the example of practical American statesmen, as opposed to British leaders who acted only on theories; it "should take a lesson from the United States, and by the adoption of a sound fiscal policy build up a great nation." As well as imitating American fiscal policy, the president of the C.M.A. said in 1888, Canada should also "cultivate the spirit" of the United States, developing in its turn a vibrant patriotism. Paradoxically, continued economic independence from the United States meant adopting Canadian national policies indistinguishable from American national policies.*[29]

---

* The other country whose industrial progress during the period deeply impressed Canadian protectionists was Germany. In its tariff and especially in its industrial education policies Germany was held up as a model for Canada at least as often as the United States. Moreover, from a Canadian vantage point it was particularly impressive that the Germans were winning their trade rivalry with England.

It also meant encouraging American investment in Canada. The branch-plant creating effect of the tariff was well-known during the period and was always hailed as one of protection's greatest achievements. From 1882 to 1896 a broken run of the *Canadian Manufacturer* contains sixty-nine references to branch-plants being considered by Americans, negotiations being carried on towards the establishment of branch-plants, branch-plants being established, and the benefits of branch-plants. Rightly or wrongly, the phenomenon was invariably explained as the result of the tariff: "Score another for the N.P.," "the N.P. does it," "more fruit from the N.P. tree," "another monument to the glory and success of our National Policy."[30] The need to protect American branch-plants – to prevent their withdrawal from Canada – was used as an argument against unrestricted reciprocity in the 1880s, in defence of the National Policy in both the 1891 and 1896 elections, and as a significant minor theme in the Conservative-protectionist defence of the National Policy in 1911. According to industrialist John Bertram in 1896, American branch-plant managers in Canada were now "the strongest protectionists we have."[31] A wide range of other Canadian policies was designed to encourage foreign, especially American, investment in Canada. These included municipal offers of bonuses to capitalists from across the line to establish in Canada, the various applications of the "manufacturing condition" to force them to cross the border, and manipulations of the Canadian Patent Act discriminating in favour of domestic manufacture.[32]

By the early 1890s Canadians were beginning to comment on the influx of American men and money. In this early debate, protectionists ranged themselves on the side of almost all foreign investment. In 1893, for example, the *Canadian Manufacturer* noted that the Montreal *Witness* was worried that American investors in Canadian iron foundries would probably be absentee owners who would take money out of the country:

As to the views of protectionists regarding the introduction into Canada of foreign capitalists and their capital, this may be said: whenever a man comes to Canada to live and to contribute in any manner to the material success of the country, he may very properly be considered a Canadian. His birthplace may be Europe, Asia, Africa, an Isle of the sea, or even the land of the Yankee, and protectionists will be ready and willing to acknowledge him a Canadian. There would be no objection to him whatever because of the place of his nativity. And the same as regards his money.

Taking issue with predictions of the Americanization of Canada through branch-plant development, the *Journal of Commerce* could not see why there would be any perceptible difference between the voting habits of Canadian and American businessmen in Canada. Each would vote for his individual interests as a businessman. "The idea that either will continue to serve the interests of his native land in preference to that of the land in which he lives, and in which his interests are vested ... falls far short of meeting the sound, economic principles which actuate either Canadian or United States businessmen to-day," Similarly, the *Monetary Times* never retracted its 1897 position that Americans in Canada "generally settle down into the most loyal Canadians, and add in every way to the stock of business ability and intelligence that characterizes our country." It directed all of its critical remarks on foreign ownership against Canadians for not being as enterprising as those businessmen from south of the border who were contributing so much to Canadian development.[33]

Canadian protectionists did perceive a grave danger that American enterprise could ravish Canada, either by destroying Canadian industries through dumping American-made goods in Canada or by denuding the country of its resources through shipping them off to the United States as unprocessed raw materials. The former was the policy of all American manufacturers located in the United States; the latter was sometimes the aim of Americans who owned timber and mineral rights in Canada and were lobbying for free trade and/or against export duties. These last were the ugly Americans in Canada, the "foreigners" who wanted to turn Canadians into hewers of wood and drawers of water, who wanted to take all the ore out of Sudbury and leave Canadians with a large hole in the ground. Canadian protectionists warned them not to expect to have Canadian policies changed for their benefit. When they invested money in Canada they should "cease to distinguish themselves as distinctively American and become Canadianized" – like other Americans who had "merged their nationality into that of Canadians."[34] These were the only times when nationalist businessmen understood that the pacifying qualities of geography would not always work miracles by themselves, that Canadianization did not automatically follow from immigration to Canada.

The National Policy interdicted the flow of goods across national boundaries, thus establishing serious barriers to increased British-Canadian trade and working against the development of practical imperialism. But it was also consciously intended to increase the international flow of capital in Canada's direction by making investment in Canadian enterprises attractive to foreigners, thus enabling Canada to import industries instead of products. All nationalities were welcome to invest in Canada, but it happened that most of the manufacturers who brought capital and entrepreneurial skill over the tariff wall were American. In this way the nationalism of the National Policy encouraged American penetration of Canadian industrial life. But insofar as their capital and skills were being put to work inside Canada for the benefit of Canadians, it was possible to argue that these businessmen and their enterprises were being Canadianized. Their activities in providing jobs for Canadian boys and in raising the "tall chimneys" of factories that would make Canada a completed modern nation were entirely consistent with the nationalism of the National Policy and were thus an integral part of classic Canadian economic nationalism.

Arguments in defence of protection had a forcefulness and effectiveness quite lacking in the attempts to legitimize domestic combines discussed in Chapter 2. The competitors being squeezed out of the market were foreigners, not Canadian producers. The tariff seemed wonderfully to stimulate employment and capital investment, and its costs were far less obvious than those of a sugar or coal combine operating within the country. Free traders could not overcome their identification with dismal theorizing, nor the identification of their doctrine with the suffering of the English poor. Before 1896 the Liberals could not overcome their identification with free traders. The protectionist vision of a manufacturing country – a diversified industrial society – was more appealing than the apparent alternative of a society of Canadian farmers, lumberjacks, and miners. Finally, the identification of the National Policy and Canadian nationalism meant that the material sacrifices the National Policy entailed could be compensated for by the psychic satisfactions of patriotism. In this one area of their many attempts to limit competition from other businessmen and other economic groups, an important wing of the business community was able to convince many Canadians that its interest and the public interest were identical.

Protectionists were too practical, however, to allow their case to rest only on its intellectual merits. They also put their principles into political practice. The Liberals were substantially correct in the 1880s in charging that the manufacturers subsidized the Conservative party in elections in return for government subsidies through the tariff schedules. The notorious "Red Parlor" was the billiard room of the Queen's Hotel in Toronto where John A. Macdonald, on his invitation, met with manufacturers before the 1882 and 1887 elections to take "energetic steps . . . to obtain united action in the maintenance and development of the National Policy." There is no doubt that campaign contributions were pledged at the Red Parlor meetings. These must have been substantial; manufacturers present in 1887 were reported to represent invested capital worth $35,000,000.[35] The manufacturers' contributions, on top of the $1,000,000 the C.P.R. poured into Conservative coffers between 1882 and 1890, might well mean that the National Policy and the transcontinental railway survived not on their merits but because the electorate was bought and paid for.[36]

When the Liberals finally gave up their quixotic struggles against the National Policy and the C.P.R. during and after the 1896 election, manufacturers enjoyed long years without having to pay for protection. "The day is past," one of them said in 1900, "when as a solid body the manufacturers of Canada will interest themselves in an election." Nonetheless, when the old issue was revived in 1911 the manufacturers once more formed their front group, the Canadian Home Market Association, and put $70,000 of their resources on the line to help win an election for protection ($15,000 of which was an unprecedented direct contribution from the C.M.A.'s reserve fund).[37]

There was nothing subtle about these tactics. The Red Parlor meetings were reported in the press and the manufacturers made no attempt to deny that their support went to the party that served their interests, only insisting that the Association itself did not participate in political campaigns. Most manufacturers frankly admitted that their first political principle was protection. When it was an issue no other political loyalty counted, and they would support the party that supported them. James Kendry, a woollen manufacturer and long-time protectionist, told the 1907 C.M.A. convention: "Whenever any Government, no matter whether it be Tory or Grit, goes against the interests of this country, I am going to vote against it. Such ought to be the policy of every one of us. . . . It may be said that I am speaking in my own interests; but I think I have a right to speak in my own interests; all the capital I have is invested in that industry." "What's the matter with the Red Parlor?" asked the *Canadian Manufacturer*, "The Red Parlor is all right!"[38]

It was all right, the mythology held, because the cause of the Red Parlor delegates was the cause of all Canadians – manufacturers, workers, farmers – working together to create a busy, self-sufficient, harmonious industrial society:

When asked what does Protection mean
    One may this answer give:
'Tis pay for work and work for pay,
    To live and to let live,
The land to till, the mine to drill,
    The forest to remove;
With all industrial wheels at work
    Our country to improve.
When each to other, hand to hand
    Will true protectors be;
One grows the grain, one makes the goods,
    Another fells the tree.

CHORUS –
Then we'll all as true Canadians
    Together stand or fall.
Let us each other then protect,
    And heaven protect us all.

With righteous cause and justest laws,
    Resources past compare,
We then should get of immigrants
    Who want to work full share;
And here to every one who came,
    While doing no one harm,
We'd give them all protection for
    Mill, forest, mine and farm.
And then by giving work to all
    In every relation,
We'd make this Canada of ours
    A most progressive nation.

It matters not how rich the soil
    Of prairie, hill or plain;
No country yet grew truly great
    By only growing grain.
So with the farmer we should have
    Also the artisan
And find all sorts of work to do
    For every lab'ring man.
Then when the stranger reaches here
    We give him not a stone;
Of old 'twas told, it was not meet
    To live by bread alone.[39]

Chapter 6

# Businessmen and the Community

The chief business of a country is to cultivate business.

*– Canadian Grocer*, 1897

Protectionist poetry was fantasizing. Canadians did not stand together as one happy family under heaven and high tariffs. Neither governments nor other major interest groups in Canadian society accepted the simple equation of business interests and the public interest. Despite the longevity of the National Policy, the political process did not seem to businessmen to result in satisfactory regard for their interests. Instead it reflected a complex struggle of groups and "classes" that baffled and frustrated business observers who came to believe that their values and interests were being denied their rightful place in Canadian community life and that they were politically disadvantaged.

Businessmen recognized two main "classes" outside the world of employers and employees. The greatest of these was the farming community – although businessmen were never quite satisfied that farming was not an industry like any other. ("I look upon the farmer as just as much of a manufacturer as any other class in the community. He converts the elements of nature into our food; the iron man converts another portion of the products of nature into a form for our use. We are all manufacturers. . . . "[1]) Whatever it was, farming was immensely important to the Canadian economy and business observers recognized this importance. There had been wonderful progress in the various industries of the country, the *Journal of Commerce* noted in 1893, "but agricultural pursuits are still the main source of livelihood, and the farming interest may well claim to be the backbone of the country." Agriculture was "the substratum of our commercial well-being," B. E. Walker told the Bank of Commerce in 1898, the same year D. R. Wilkie told the Canadian Bankers' Association that Canada was "essentially an agricultural country." The tremendous expansion of agriculture on the Prairies after 1900 increased this sense of dependence on farming. Business journals paid close attention to the reports of each year's crop, realizing that if the harvest was bad "there will necessarily be a heavy decrease in sales. . . . Every employer and employee in the towns and cities are subject, in a greater or less degree, to the conditions as governing the farmer." In 1906 the leading organ of Canada's manufacturing interests spelled out what in the Canadian context could hardly be called an agrarian myth:

> Canada is and always will be a great agricultural country. Her mines may become exhausted, her great watersheds may be denuded of their forest growth, her fisheries are year by year being perpetuated with increasing difficulty, but her soil will be perennially productive. Farm property is undoubtedly her greatest and most permanent asset. It is the farm that builds her railway and steamship lines, her telegraph and telephone lines. Without the farmer Canada's trade and commerce would be as a house built upon sand. He is the very foundation stone of our social economy. His barns are the measure of our country's prosperity.[2]

Acting on these premises, businessmen were ardent promoters of agricultural development. Anything that enabled the farmer to produce more and better products – "to make two blades of grass grow where formerly was but one" – was considered "a benefaction to mankind" and to Canadian prosperity.[3] The business press enthusiastically supported experimental farms, agricultural colleges, dairy programmes, etc., never begrudging any public expenditure in this direction. Business journals bombarded farmers with detailed advice on every conceivable aspect of their occupation – butter-making, soil fertilization, crop rotation, methods of cutting weeds, tree-planting, the need to keep accounts, etc. Their main interest was to encourage farmers to maximize their productivity and efficiency by the use of the most advanced techniques and equipment. Modern farming was referred to as a "business," a "science," and even a "learned profession." Where farmers were backwards and unprogressive, notably in Quebec, they were roundly condemned for their conservatism. "L'Indolence et l'Insouciance des Populations Agricoles" was a favourite theme of *Le Moniteur du Commerce* as it chastised the farmer who dumbly cultivated as his great-grandfathers had, spent his income on luxuries, paid no attention to the ever-changing and ever-demanding requirements of successful farming, and then, when he failed, meekly gave up and went off to wage-slavery in American factories.

On the other hand, the farmer who was progressive, hard-working and thrifty – "homme véritablement d'affaires" – would always prosper.[4]

In fact, *Le Moniteur du Commerce* thought Quebec's pressing need was for more farmers, and was a highly enthusiastic supporter of the colonization movement. It routinely reprinted colonization literature complete with the slogan, "Emparons-nous du sol," discouraged young men from leaving the land (especially if they planned to enter the swollen ranks of small merchants), and was led into formulations of agrarian mythology as grandiose as any that farmers themselves produced: "Croyez-nous, cultivateurs, l'homme le plus heureux de la terre est le cultivateur qui ne doit pas un sou à personne et qui tient sa ferme en bon état de culture . . . à tout considérer, l'état de cultivateur est celui qui est le plus prospère. De toutes les classes de la société, le cultivateur est le plus libre, le plus indépendent, et celui qui retire le plus de profit de son travail."[5]

These attitudes were not unique to the French-Canadian business paper. English-Canadian businessmen, who, of course, enthusiastically encouraged the "colonization" of the Western prairies, also puzzled over the "rush to the cities" to dreary occupations "in which no man is his own master."[6] Straying farmers were criticized for not understanding the intellectual challenge of their profession, for not appreciating the genuine independence it offered, and for not realizing that "there is no class of men with the same capital and with the same activity and brain work who have accumulated so much . . . as those who have been farmers who put some brains into their business."[7] Agriculture, they thought, was the one industry that could take up any slack in employment and turn the urban poor into useful members of the labour force. That is why Canada's leading business paper, the *Monetary Times,* would publish an editorial in the 1907 recession entitled "Back to the Land."[8]

It was particularly desirable that young men should stay on the land rather than join the other major "class" in Canadian society, members of the liberal professions – lawyers, teachers, doctors, and clergymen. Almost all comment about the professions emphasized that there were more professional people than the country needed. Noticing the problem of "Unemployed Churchmen," for example, the *Canadian Manufacturer* portrayed the professions in general as a haven for the lazy and unenterprising:

In truth, these professions are the refuge of a large class of incompetent and useless men who are too lazy and too puffed up with vain conceit to ever do an honest day's work, depending on the *éclat* that surrounds professional life to supply the dupes who are to support them in refined and elegant ease. And when the pinching of want is felt they discover that they are ignorant as to how to earn honest bread.

If the mythology surrounding the professions were stripped away it would be found that as much or more was contributed to the community by the honest workman as by the rowdy young men in the universities who soon joined the ranks of the "non-producing" classes:

A good blacksmith is of more value to the country than a score of clerical students who have devoted years of their lives to the study of theology, but who can never hope to be even shepherds without flocks; but who might have earned honest bread by swinging a sledge hammer. A good machinist, capable to grind a valve seat or fit a key is worth a regiment of professional lawyers; and a miller who knows how to convert wheat into flour, or a farmer who knows how to cultivate wheat, is worth more than all the incipient sawbones turned out of the medical colleges, and licensed to kill or cure, as the fates may determine.[9]

The *Canadian Manufacturer* often shouted what other business papers whispered, but nagging resentment at the liberal professions and their privileges was general and part of an extensive business belief that priorities were being turned around in Canadian society. The *Monetary Times* was upset at the disdain of young would-be professionals for manual labour and felt that their attitudes reflected the North American search for easy success. A C.M.A. resolution in 1900 deplored the tendency of Canadian higher education to fit men only for the "so-called" professions. Testifying before the Royal Commission on Technical Education in 1912, a deputation from the Toronto Board of Trade complained about the element in the universities who were being trained to despise commercial and industrial life, students who did not realize that the captains of industry "are just as great in the sight of Providence and in the sight of the nation as men in some of the professions."[10]

The occasional analysis blamed the value system of Canadian society in general for this unhappy state of affairs,* but more commonly criticism centred on the way the educational system fostered these wrong priorities. As D. R. Wilkie told the Canadian

* "How many of our well-to-do families follow the wise example set in the highest places in Germany, by sending their sons after the college days are over to

Bankers' Association in 1898, it was a system that wasted months and years in "the indiscriminate study of algebra and mathematics and the dead languages," which had no conceivable value to the real world of experience and earning a living. The *Dry Goods Review* though the real school question in the 1890s should be the way that schools filled pupils "with sciences and arts and 'ologies so that they are ashamed of honest toil." "As to all the practical affairs of daily life," the *Journal of Comerce* grumbled, "the minds of the vast numbers of those who have gone through our high schools and universities are usually as blank as though they had been trained on a distant star." The *Canadian Manufacturer* was particularly upset at the injustice of taxing manufacturers and their employees to pay the costs of educating rich men's children at collegiates and universities, thereby unfitting them for practical pursuits and turning them into professionals "for which the country has no possible use." The business interest in education being more practical, more geared to instilling ordinary skills and turning out trained working people, does much to explain the business community's unanimous support for technical and vocational education.[11]

The clash with professionals and their values was sharpest in the province of Quebec where *Le Moniteur du Commerce*, speaking for the small French-Canadian business community, was convinced that the dominance of the liberal professions explained the lack of French-Canadian business prowess. "Ces carrières ont tellement tourné la tête à notre jeunesse depuis quarante ans, qu'elle a avec les familles, oublié que l'on pouvait être agronome éminent, chimiste savant, ingénieur civil compétent dans les chemins de fer, les mines, les routes, la marine, les canaux, etc., à ce point que les meilleures positions, les emplois les plus lucratifs, commes les plus honorables, sont confiés à des mains étrangères, pour la bonne raison que notre jeunesse canadienne française a dédaigné de s'en occuper."[12]

Controlling the school system as they did, the professions in

---

learn a trade, to get some knowledge of, say, cotton or woollen manufacturing, furniture making, house-building, plumbing, etc.? The young men themselves rarely look upon such employment with any sort of favor. The consequence is that when a new cotton mill or other manufactory is started, the man capable of managing it must be imported; . . . It is not, of course, considered the thing for those who move in the higher circles in our towns and cities to engage in employments where manual labour is necessary; – it is deemed preferable to compete for the few situations in banks and counting houses, even in the retail stores, for the lowest remunerations, or starve in law offices, or seek any other half paid and precarious employment rather than seek good wages, advancement, and probable wealth, by learning some useful mechanical occupation." (*Journal of Commerce*, July 1883, p. 1612.)

Quebec were thought to perpetuate themselves by offering an education centering on "les langues mortes" which destroyed any possible student interest in or competence at the affairs of business. "Ils n'ont pas la moindre idée de ce que c'est qu'une facture de marchandise ou une quittance, ils sont incapables d'écrire une lettre convenablement, leur calligraphie est hyéroglifique et la langue anglaise leur est en horreur." What was needed in Quebec, the editors felt, was a radical change in the whole primary school system ("de porter la hache et la cognée dans le vieil édifice qui entrave l'essor des générations présentes et qui met notre race dans état d'infériorité douloureuse vis-à-vis de ses concurrents") that would necessarily involve ending the Church's control of education. Indeed, in the Quebec milieu it would involve a fairly considerable attack on the values of the Church because they were so antithetical to the affairs of the modern world. What else could one do with a system dominated by clerics whose main aim was to teach students "que le monde où les trois quarts vont s'engouffrer n'est que l'anti-chambre de l'enfer, un mode odieux au milieu duquel il faut vivre en se refusant toutes les jouissances honnêtes, fermer les yeux à tout progrès matériel parce que le matérialisme y domine, vivre de pain d'orge et d'eau, faire imprimer ses blancs de reçus et de comptes, et faire confectionner ses chemises dans un établissement de réligieux pour rester honnête citoyen"?*[13]

Businessmen felt that the other "classes" in the community had a distressing tendency to use the political system for their own selfish ends. Chapter 4 discussed businessmen's resentment

---

\* Insofar as it reflected this world view, traditional French-Canadian nationalism could not be identified with French-Canadian business interests in the way that English-Canadian nationalism and tariff protection were linked. *Le Moniteur du Commerce,* the leading French-Canadian business journal, was instead concerned that the traditional patriotism of the St. Jean Baptiste Day variety led too often to a timid exclusionism, a refusal to have anything to do with North Americans that reinforced Quebec's isolation from the mainstream of North American business and strengthened clerical and professional domination of French-Canadian society. Although the journal was a stout defender of the French language and French culture in North America, it nevertheless believed strongly that nationalism should not intrude on business. "Dans le domaine du commerce, de l'industrie, de l'agriculture, de la navigation, etc., il ne doit pas exister de nationalité distincte en Canada, ou plutôt, il ne doit y exister qu'une seule nationalité, 'la nationalité canadienne'." It believed that French-Canadians were not discriminated against in business and gave no shrift to proposals for counter-discrimination such as the idea of French-Canadians patronizing businessmen of their own nationality. "Si un pharmacien anglais vous offrait un article de médecin dix pour cent meilleur marché que l'offrirait un pharmacien canadien-français, que feriez-vous?" the editor asked. To a true businessman the answer was obvious. (3 déc., 1888, p. 524.)

at the tendency of their workingmen to organize themselves into unions to avoid or lessen their duties. They were even more distressed to realize how quickly organized labour had learned the uses of politics and the arts of lobbying, and how receptive politicians were to the implications of the labour vote. As early as 1882 the *Monetary Times* had complained about Ontario's having extended "special privileges" to labour that were unjust to other interests. In 1888 the *Journal of Commerce* felt that "the future of the artisan fills the whole horizon of politics and no other class is considered at all."[14] When Parliament began to make highly visible responses to labour pressure after 1900 – establishing a Department of Labour, founding the *Labour Gazette,* introducing fair wage provisions into federal works contracts, and giving a friendly hearing to bills to institute the eight-hour day on Dominion public works – employers were enraged at how politicians had abandoned impartiality "for fear of offending organized labor, and in order to secure patronage."[15] The C.M.A.'s Parliamentary Committee described the political struggle in 1906 this way:

> Trade unionism has continued to follow an aggressive course in seeking to further its own interests at the expense of the community at large. . . . Labor agitators have been steadily at work, clamoring for the enactment of class legislation, and endeavoring to enlist the support of members of both political parties. . . . That legislators, in order to obtain favour with unincorporated bodies, who have steadily declined to assume their lawful responsibilities, should adopt measures which react upon those whose interests are centred in the upbuilding of the nation, indicates a regrettable degree of weakness, and points to the necessity for vigorous and concerted action by the employing classes if they are to protect their own.[16]

The farmers also showed a tendency to behave much the same way as workers. Instead of sticking to farming they continually tried to improve their lot by unreasoning and unproductive attacks on their fellow businessmen. Agrarian organizations and political activity from the formation of the Manitoba Farmers' Union through the campaign for reciprocity of 1910-11 were interpreted in almost exactly the same categories as the trade-union movement. Agitators, usually self-interested, played on the farmer's credulity and irrationality to drive a wedge between agrarians and their natural allies in the commercial community. Very upset at Nationalist politics in Quebec in the late 1880s, particularly the imposition of taxes on corporations, the *Journal of Commerce* complained that "the whole of the electoral power is held by ignorant and bigoted

French-Canadian farmers who believe everything that a glib-tongued orator of their own race and creed chooses to tell them, and who care nothing for the advancement of the country so long as their own little farms are not taxed." By 1909 the *Financial Post*'s Western correspondent, covering the establishment of publicly owned grain elevators hard on the heels of attacks on the Winnipeg Grain Exchange, called wistfully for "strong statesmen of sufficient breadth of view and foresight" to stem the "tide of privileged legis-lation and the encouragement of a tyrannical 'upper class' " (i.e. farmers) that was sweeping the Prairies. When the C.M.A. held its private tariff strategy discussions in 1910 and 1911 there were the usual outbursts: it "seemed that the farmer was naturally favoura-bly regarded by Governments"; the "whole trend of the Govern-ment's policy seemed to be to set the farmer against the manufac-turer, to uphold agriculture at the expense of every other industry"; if the Association wanted to have its policy accepted it would have to work through "channels that carry influence at Ottawa, that is to say through the farmers and through the working classes."[17]

Frustration at the "unreasonable" complaints and political activities of farmers could occasion anti-agrarian sentiments which more than countered the glowing tributes to the impor-tance of agriculture and the merits of farming as a profession. Believing that Western Canadians had been lavishly subsidized with free land, railways built by Eastern money, etc., B. E. Walker could only conclude that "The attitude of the West regarding eleva-tors, freight rates, free trade, etc., etc., is quite natural when one remembers that agricultural people as a rule are both selfish and ignorant." When the *Journal of Commerce*, after years of resent-ment at the rural-dominated Quebec legislature. saw agrarian agi-tation mounting all across Canada in the 1890s, it lost all patience with farmers and their self-image:

It is the misfortune of the farmer that those to whom he is most ready to listen have contented themselves with playing on his vanity and credulity in order to attain their ends instead of endeavoring to educate him in the broader principles of statesmanship. He has been so satiated with flattery that he has come to believe that honesty, truth and integrity are qualities principally engendered by actual contact with the soil. His covetousness is glossed over as thrift, his stupidity becomes innocence, and his jealousy and narrow mindedness are dignified as the natural watchfulness of a pure nature against the contamination of town life. In fact he is an ideal-ized farmer – something that never did, and never will exist,

121

except in the imagination of the country orator. It is no wonder, then, that he deems himself the salt of the earth, the reformer of the evils brought about by the capitalist and the manufacturer, or that, buoyed up by these false impressions, he plunges into the extravagances which are rapidly bringing the populist party in the United States into disrepute. In fact it is only because he is too busy looking after his own interests to bother other people that he has not interfered more with the progress of the country than he has, and thus his innate selfishness has proved a distinct benefit to the community at large.[18]

For the most part businessmen did not perceive any serious threat to the Canadian community from anyone further to the left than union and farm leaders. Although the business press was aware of the activities of communists, nihilists, and anarchists in other countries, and generally understood what socialism was about, there was little feeling that these most extreme critics of the social order were responsible for Canadian problems. True, for years the *Monetary Times* carried on a running war against those preachers of "the gospel of confiscation," the Single Taxers ("for single tax it is difficult to see how any right-minded person can have any other feeling than that of loathing and contempt"). The *Journal of Commerce* was unimpressed with "that class of long-haired men and short-haired women who are always anxious to do good at other people's expense, provided they can see some prospect of advertising themselves and their particular 'isms thereby." And there were occasional complaints about the irresponsibility of newspapers and the soft-headedness of clergymen spouting Single Tax or other "wild and preposterous theories picked out of the gutter of romance literature."[19] But Canada had no Haymarket bombers or organized anarchists, and such isolated incidents as the appearance of black flags in parades of Toronto unemployed could be sloughed off as insignificant.[20] At an executive session of the C.M.A. in 1907 one alarmist manufacturer raised the issue of socialist agitators speaking freely in Toronto parks, and suggested that the Association alert the government to the matter. But John Northway declared "that it would be a decided mistake in policy for the Association to attempt in any way to curb free speech"; the sense of the meeting was that "agitation of this kind would accomplish very little ultimately, and the socialists if left alone would ruin their own cause." It was only under the extreme provocation of the Glace Bay strike of 1909 that the normally balanced editors of the *Canadian Mining Journal* branded the "majority" of North American labour leaders as "demagogues, imbued with the dogmata of a crude form of socialism, which is in reality a variant of anarchism modified by opportunism and illiteracy."[21]

Most of what was wrong with the state of Canadian politics could most appropriately be blamed on the people who pandered to the tendencies of labour and farmers to demand special favours, i.e. on the politicians who pandered to their votes. Governments usually behaved badly, businessmen thought, and their comments on the methods and priorities of politicians were uniformly critical. Their attention to politics varied with the fortunes of the economy and the apparent efficiency of Canadian governments. Anti-political sentiment produced an extraordinarily broad wave of critical comment in the 1890s, but tapered off considerably in the prosperity after 1900. Even then businessmen periodically reminded each other that politicians were all a bad lot and the best to be said was that the country was prospering in spite of them.

Aside from their corruption and inefficiency, serious enough problems in themselves, the basic trouble with governments was that they were not responsive enough to business interests. Employers felt that virtually the whole legislative programme put forward by organized labour and any favourable political response to it represented an attack on business interests. The insistence of agrarians on continuing the assault on the National Policy meant that protectionists could never be secure in their enjoyment of high tariffs, but continually had to intervene in elections, with all the temporary insecurity that meant, to defend policies that should be beyond dispute. In the middle 1890s another group received far too much political attention – the "cranks who place religious prejudices above everthing else" (according to the *Canadian Manufacturer*) kept Parliament in session for months on end discussing the Manitoba Schools problem while the business affairs of the country were stagnating in neglect.[22]

A pessimistic explanation of the failures of government concentrated on the flaws of democracy. The very conservative *Journal of Commerce* equated the extension of the franchise with republican political institutions and announced in 1890 that "the political tendency of a republican form of government ... must inevitably be towards corruption." In Quebec, it felt, the balance of political power was now in the hands of French-Canadian *habitants*, "an industrious race, and one frugal almost to penuriousness; but ignorant, superstitious, intolerant and bigoted, and therefore falling easily under the sway of any facile or unscrupulous politician who may appeal to their racial or religious prejudices to carry him into power." Things were better in Ontario, but even there the balance of power was held by "the

123

most ignorant of the population." The result of the working of democracy in both provinces had been

> the formation of a class of professional politicians who seek to enter parliament for the deliberate purpose of obtaining wealth thereby. Confident in the possession of the necessary "pull" and in the interested adherence of the "bosses" and "heelers" who control the great mass of their constituents, the moment they are elected they proceed to seek opportunities of inserting their hands into the national coffers. Should they be successful, they are regarded with mingled admiration and envy by those who have neither the impudence nor the opportunity to follow their example. Should they fail, they turn unabashed to their constituency and trust by lavish promises of the expenditure of public money (and possibly a judicious distribution of their own) to be once more placed in a position to secure a share of the "boodle".

This situation was the result of "the confiding of the future of this country to the hands of the poorest and most ignorant, and therefore most numerous, class of its population . . . the setting up of the rule of a brute majority over an educated and intelligent minority."[23]

Much more commonly, business critics of government concentrated on the background of politicians. Far too many of them were drawn from the liberal professions: doctors, teachers, and, above all, lawyers. At best men with professional training were incapable of looking after business interests or running a businesslike government. Lawyers, for instance, created most of the cumbrous machinery of the law because "they cannot see that a plain, business-like system, with no unnecessary waste of time and money, is the best system for for us."[24] The proper sphere of doctors was prescribing for overfed urchins; and a "schoolmaster" like Finance Minister Foster seemed in 1895 more suited to being a Minister of Education in a provincial government. In the climate of the 1890s most of these professionals seemed to be "men who were more at home discussing such questions as to whether a candidate for baptism should be baptised in a tub or in a lake, than discerning a fine point in business ethics. Men who were more at home stirring up sectarian strife than devising ways and means of building up the trade of the country. Men who could devote years of their lives to feeding the fires of racial animosity and not one hour to the work of propagating the seeds of nationalism and good will."[25]

In addition to being naturally incompetent at the business of politics, professional men were too apt to turn into, if they were not already, professional politicians. Many of the professionals who went into politics were failures in their overcrowded professions – "the sediment of the learned professions" – who drifted into politics, the one occupation which did not require special training, because it was "the best paying job which their mediocrity will allow them to obtain."[26] Once in office they bent all their energies to staying there. They made politics their profession, the sole aim being to make what they could get out of it. Governments, many business observers felt, were little more than organized gangs of professional politicians who kept their political machines – the political parties – going by dispensing loot and jobs from the public treasury. If this situation were allowed to continue the influence of merchants in public affairs would continue to decline, "until we are simply hewers of wood and drawers of water for the professional politicians . . . [who are] a class of hacks and heelers." "Les politiciens de profession! Voilà l'ennemi à combattre!"[27]

The obvious solution to this failure of government to meet the needs of "the most important class in the community" was for more members of that class to go into government. A business presence in government, it was thought, would almost by definition be a force for reform and good government. Businessmen possessed the ability to administer political institutions efficiently; successful men of affairs would, by virtue of their wealth, be insulated from financial temptation, being in politics only to serve not to steal. Putting "country before party," they would run the nation's business on the same principles as they ran their own private businesses. Thus the *Commercial* called upon the Winnipeg electorate to place the affairs of the city "upon a basis as nearly as possible similar to that which obtains in the conduct of any large business enterprise"; the Maclean trade journals in the 1890s printed lists of businessmen running for public office and urged their readers to give them support; the Toronto Branch of the Canadian Manufacturers' Association discussed tactics for increasing the business representation in city politics; and in the 1911 election the *Journal of Commerce* told politicians to go away:

The overwhelming proportion of second-rate lawyers and professional politicians might be asked to stand aside at this important election. Great captains of industry, leaders in the broadest field of commerce, heads of large corporations would be welcome among the candidates. A grave business question is up for consideration, and business men of large experience and high standing should deal with it. It is not a time for the

TO THE RESCUE!
Or, Miss Canada in the clutches of the foul fiend of corruption.

glibness of the hired talker, or the needy place seeker. It will be a mistake if it is left to the ordinary political heelers to attend to this matter.[28]

Most businessmen complained about politics and did nothing. Much of the complaining, in fact, was about the refusal of businessmen to do something about the political mess everyone complained about. Many of the wealthy seemed to prefer to attend to their own business and even permit themselves to be "robbed a little by bad laws and bad men" rather than give their time to legislation. But perhaps this was an understandable reaction to the politics of the new democracy. As a correspondent wrote to the *Monetary Times*, "A citizen of sterling integrity and manly principle will decline to go from house to house, side-line to side-line, hat in hand, begging a vote from 'Tom, Dick and Harry,' kissing babies, and playing the role of conscious hypocrisy. Every time he is compelled by custom to adopt such methods, he will feel his manhood shrink; until, finally, it may be entirely extinguished, and he becomes a full-fledged professional politician."[29] The would-be Cincinnatus in the business community would only put down his tools to govern, not to engage in politics.

If politics could not literally be taken over by businessmen then perhaps the important business issues could be taken out of the hands of politicians. The *Commercial* suggested that an "advisory board or committee" might be formed from the leading Boards of Trade in the country which would have the privilege of suggesting "required" legislation to Parliament and consulting with it on business matters. The *Canadian Grocer* advocated settling the matter of Newfoundland's joining Canada ("emphatically" a business issue) by having a commission of businessmen examine the Island's resources and decide on the merits of union as a commercial transaction. Above all, most of the manufacturers thought the tariff should be taken out of Canadian politics forever by turning tariff matters over to a commission or board of experts who would set a "scientific" or "business-like" tariff.* A

---

\* This proposal was first heard in the 1890s when manufacturers were faced with the likelihood of a Liberal government attacking the National Policy. It was revived again in 1903-1904 and 1908-1910. Of course a "scientific" or "business-like" tariff would be highly protectionist. But the C.M.A.'s Tariff Committee abruptly dropped the idea in 1910 when it decided that protectionist sentiment in the country was so weak that any tariff commission established by the government would consist of members mostly unsympathetic to protection. In these circumstances it seemed best to hold governments "absolutely responsible" for tariff changes so that protectionists would at least have political recourse to defend their interests.

crusty old banker, Thomas Fyshe, took these notions to their extreme in a 1907 article in the *Journal of the Canadian Bankers' Association,* arguing that, since government was the one institution in society which could be relied on never to achieve anything of value, all of the charitable and educational institutions of the community should be turned over to the joint-stock companies, making them totally responsible for the moral and material well-being of their employees. It was a call for the effectual withering away of the state.[30]

Most of these proposals were grossly impractical, at least on anything but the municipal level (where the impact of business ideas of managerial efficiency was reflected in reformers' interest in turning many of the duties of municipal councils over to appointed administrative bodies). Aside from protesting and lobbying against what seemed to be the more outrageous acts of government, the only other non-partisan recourse businessmen had to objectionable legislation was to threaten to go away angry, or bankrupt, or both. The danger that manufacturers would close their plants had always lurked in the background of tariff discussions. It surfaced most clearly during the 1896 election when die-hard Tory manufacturers told their hands that their factories would be closed if a Liberal government were elected, and immediately afterwards when the *Canadian Manufacturer* tried to put pressure on the new government by printing a long list of factories laying off their men, closing down, postponing investments, and so on, under the heading, "Laurier, Mowat, and Misery." Higher taxes were always objected to as sure to kill "the goose that lays the golden eggs" ("upon its delicate organization taxation acts literally like the hand of death. It shrinks, withers or dies at the touch"). In the struggle to establish Ontario Hydro, Premier Whitney of Ontario had to overcome a concerted effort by the private power interests to ruin the credit of his province in the English money markets. The British Columbia Electric Railway in its disputes with the government of that province threatened to reduce company expenditures and warned that hostile legislation "means absolutely not a penny of British capital for all Vancouver enterprises for four to five years." In these and all other situations the investment climate had to be kept as favourable as possible to induce timid capitalists to keep on risking their wealth, that delicate goose to go on laying. If the "captain of industry" was a valuable asset to the community because of the capital and skills he brought to it, his final weapon in disputes with authorities who controlled the coercive power of law, or with voters who outnumbered him at the polls, was to threaten to take his capital and skills and go home.[31]

But that was an extreme and unpleasant recourse, often only a bluff because it might cost the interested party much more than he stood to gain. Perhaps the most common response to a difficult political situation was simple partisan action. When the chips were down in politics, on, say, protection or the future of transcontinental railways, there was nothing to do but offer support, mostly financial, to the political party that best represented one's interests. The two classic instances of this were the manufacturers' support of the Conservatives before 1896 as the party of tariff protection and the C.P.R.'s support of the same party in the 1880s. But getting involved in partisan politics had its share of perils for the businessman or business organization. Aside from being expensive, taking political sides opened the way to vindictive retribution if the opposition won. It meant openly courting public opinion, a weak reed at best; and in the case of the C.M.A. and protection involved having to soften one's stand on other issues to continue to be able to court public support.* As well, there was the difficulty of conflicting business interests cancelling out one's own efforts.

The truth was that on most political issues businessmen differed sharply. In the great railway struggles of the 1880s and 1890s one of the main sources of the C.P.R.'s insecurity in its relationship with the Canadian Government was the Grand Trunk Railway's support for the Opposition. When shippers

* In both 1901 and 1908 the C.M.A. explicitly rejected adopting an open anti-labour policy, which would have meant forming a Labor Department to co-ordinate anti-union activities, because it did not want to be cast as an anti-labour organization. Such an image, the executive decided, "would tend to lessen its influence to a great extent throughout the Dominion." (Minutes, Sept. 18, 1902.) A 1909 proposal that the Association challenge the Ontario Factory Act on constitutional grounds because a member wanted to put on a night shift of women never got past the committee stage. The feeling was that "it would be unwise for the Association to raise the question of employing females at night, as the practice would not meet with the public approval." (Parliamentary Committee, Minutes, Feb. 17, 1909.) The same year, the Toronto Branch modified a scheme for lobbying against a provincial fair wages bill because of "the danger of publicity as a result of such a step being taken." (Minutes, March 11, 1909.) And in 1907-1908, the Association had been badly bruised by charges that it was importing strikebreakers through its British office. It had taken pains not to lay itself open to such criticism ("The feeling of the committee was that the Association should be very careful to do nothing which might give color to the accusation that they were in business as strikebreakers" British Office, Committee Minutes, Dec. 3, 1907) but it had been trapped by a combination of bad timing and the incompetence of the British agent. At all times in its history the manufacturers' association did everything it could to maintain at least the veneer of non-partisanship and would have appreciated nothing more than being able to withdraw from partisan political activity.

who felt discriminated against by railway rates called for much tighter government regulation of both systems their efforts were nullified by an alliance of the railways with those shippers who did not feel discriminated against (the only point of agreement among all parties was that any regulatory agency which might be set up had to be absolutely non-political).[32] Protectionist business-men were always bedevilled, or thought they were, by the free-trade "fifth column" in their midst working in alliance with agrarian interests against the National Policy.* Indeed, the unity of protec-tionists themselves on the structure of the tariff was always very fragile and seems to have largely disintegrated before the Fielding inquiry of 1905.[33] Twenty-five years of mercantile agitation for a federal insolvency law led nowhere, mainly because of business ina-bility to agree on a law that would satisfy all the competing inter-ests.[34] And there was a massive area of business agitation and com-petition for government favours that has not been touched on in this study: the struggles of businessmen organized in their Boards of Trade to advance the interests of each locality against all others – a kind of war of all against all that in passing created much of the sound and fury of Canadian regionalism.

There was no coherent philosophy in the business community that could specify the task of government in a given situation. Every businessmen who found that government could promote his interests favoured active government. Every promoter, for example, who had a chance to get a subsidy thought it proper for governments to make a venture less hazardous by generous encouragement. Manufacturers gave no thought to the "paternal-ist" implications of the tariff or of asking the state to train their workers and develop export markets for their products. As con-sumers many businessmen wanted government regulation and/ or ownership of public utilities in the interests of obtaining cheap, efficient light, water, power, telephone, and transportation systems. The drive for government assistance in cost reduction reached its peak in Ontario in the early years of the twentieth century when a businessmen's movement produced the provin-cially owned hydro-electric system, utterly misnamed by some as "The People's Power." The private power interests cried foul confiscation, socialism, the abolition of Magna Carta, and the destruction of Canada's credit. They stood on every principle

* As late as 1910 the Tariff Committee of the C.M.A. privately decided that the bulk of the agitation against protection originated with large importing firms "having alliances with foreign producers, all done with a view of advancing their own personal interests and being quite willing to exploit both the manu-facturer and the consumer" (Tariff Committee. Minutes. March 16, 1910).

ever devised to explain why government should not compete with private enterprise. But what did a few vested interests weigh in the overall balance? "The matter of ownership ... is but of secondary importance to the Toronto manufacturers, the great consideration with them being cheap power and light. ... "[39]

The manufacturers who cheered on the attack on the private power interests had little use for some other aspects of municipal regulation. Smoke by-laws and building codes, for example, gravely interfered with their own businesses. If these were not exactly illegitimate extensions of state power, they were certainly unnecessary regulations whose harmful effects would be evident when enterprise fled from the city.[36] Nor would it be fair of the Federal Government to raise manufacturers' insurance costs by granting Canadian underwriters the same kind of protection from foreign competition that manufacturers were currently enjoying. Protection for fire insurance companies would mean the legitimization of a monopoly, they charged, one which employed very few men and contributed nothing essential to the national production.[37] Municipal and federal bonuses were a useful stimulant to the enterprise of the firm that received the bonuses; but to established firms competing with the bonusee it was wasteful, unfair, even "the grossest communism," and should be abolished by law.[38] John A. Macdonald received many complaints from the Grand Trunk during the 1880s about public money being used to create competition with railways built by private capital "to which the country has not contributed a single dollar." In 1888 Stephen of the C.P.R. also suggested to him that the time had come to stop giving subsidies to railways![39]

It was even difficult to achieve consensus on what seemed to be fundamental or transcendental questions involving business liberty or the rights of private property. Extremists on the labour question could not move the C.M.A. to support them because it had to protect its public image to preserve the National Policy. When the Retail Merchants' Association was lobbying for amendments to the Criminal Code to legalize price-fixing, the C.M.A. refused to co-operate for fear of disrupting existing arrangements.[40] The private power people in Ontario thought the government was upsetting the foundation of private enterprise and striking at the roots of civil society to boot. Manufacturers ignored them as they lusted after cheap power. What was life and death and a matter of the highest principle to one businessman was often a mere side issue to another.

Sometimes circumstances dictated taking several positions simultaneously. A British Columbia mine manager told his branch of the Canadian Mining Institute that the industry required nothing but the abolition of bad laws. "All it wants from the State is what Diogenes asked from Alexander, 'keep out of my sunlight'." The bad laws, of course, were all those levying taxes on the industry. But he went on to claim that the state should also "encourage and aid" the industry by "attending to all those matters which are beyond private enterprise"; and thought the Department of Mines should be the industry's "representative, its advocate and its watchful guardian." The *Journal of Commerce* perhaps took the prize for simultaneously maintaining contradictory theories of government when it answered a correspondent who thought it odd that the journal should condemn the establishment of a Department of Labour to advance the interests of the working classes in the same issue that it was asking for government aid to protect Montreal from discriminatory interest rates:

> Our correspondent fails to see the vital difference between a government coddling workingmen by taking their trades unions under its wing, which they can, as they ought to, manage without government help, and a government using its powers to protect a shipping port from what is regarded by many as a movement to do it serious injury. Governments interfere with all classes, but, when a government voluntarily takes an active part in managing the affairs of trades unions, it takes work in hand which is wholly outside its province and this meddling weakens the self-reliance and title to self-respect of those upon whom it obtrudes its help. On the other hand, when a government exercises its influence to guard the national port from what is threatening to do that port very serious damage, it is fulfilling a natural function of government. In one case it is coddling a class without any reason, and in the other it is exercising the supreme influence of a government in the general interests of the country.[41]

Businessmen attempted to manipulate the various levels of government just as pragmatically as they wielded political theory. What provinces held back, in the way of subsidies, for example, municipalities might offer, and vice versa. If circumstances prevented the Federal Government from applying the manufacturing condition, perhaps the provinces could levy export licenses. A provincial government could do yeoman service by controlling municipalities on the one hand and championing regional interests against Ottawa on the other. Then again, Ottawa had the power of disallowance, such a useful tool when provinces behaved irresponsibly (and, in the case of Ontario with hydro, managed to assert their supremacy over that last line of defence of business rights, the courts).[42] In 1885, when the Winnipeg Board of Trade was in the thick of the fight against Ottawa's use of disallowance to maintain the C.P.R.'s monopoly clause, the Manitoba legislature passed a law retroactively exempting certain properties of a debtor from seizure by his creditors. The Board immediately petitioned the Governor-General to have the Act disallowed. A letter to the *Commercial* wondering at the inconsistency of the Board was given "the simple answer that in both instances the Board acted in the best interests of trade, and did not so much as trouble itself to enquire into the political bearings of either question." Those Winnipegers who did not understand this were "unfit to take part in the deliberations of the Board of Trade, for the simple reason that they place political hobbies and bigotry before the interests of trade."[43]

It was true that businessmen had in common a desire to see businessmen and business principles instilled in government. This, however, only masked the conflict which appeared when issues were specified. One businessman could want businessmen in government to frustrate the schemes of demagogic politicians for socialization of industries; another businessman might want politics to become more businesslike so that governments would have the administrative talent to run the franchises he thought should be expropriated. The "class" interests of businessmen only dictated that each businessman would expect government to abide by his fairly fluid concept of business principles. When it was time to sit down and iron out disagreements in principle among businessmen it was found that they were locked in deadly competition.

# Conclusion

The previous six chapters have set out businessmen's ideas on a number of business and social problems. Large chunks of the material beg a basic question: does any of this matter? Were the expressed opinions of businessmen and their spokesmen in the business papers any more than crude rationalizations for actions in the real world which reflected quite different aims and ideas? In Chapters 1 and 2, for example, it was shown that the rhetoric of individualism in business was supplemented in practice by very considerable collectivism to minimize the impact of competition. Does that mean that the rhetoric was useless dross that no one took seriously? Similarly, were protestations of concern for the workingman's welfare and charges that trade unions operated against the worker's best interests no more than verbal smoke-screens masking calculated exploitation of the worker and destruction of his organizations? Was the defence of protection no more than a manipulation of nationalism in the interests of higher profits? Were complaints about the lack of business influence in government absurd and misleading whining from a class who in fact pulled the strings of Canadian politics? In short, can anything be gleaned from a study of business ideas unless they are contrasted with the reality of business practice? And would that study not lead us quickly back to the notion that being in business was about nothing more than making as much money as fast as possible?

One extreme and untenable answer to these questions would be that all the ideas set out here accurately reflect the beliefs of all businessmen, who all acted upon these beliefs. This is untenable on the general ground that no group in society ever perfectly implements its values and ideals; all groups, even university professors, have their share of liars, cheats, and cynics whose careers belie the mystique of their profession. More specifically, it would fly in the face of hard evidence, a good deal of which has been presented here, and simple common sense to describe a

business community peopled only by thrifty, industrious entrepreneurs solicitous of their workingmen and customers, dedicated to the building of the Canadian nation, and genuinely
alienated from a society that paid little attention to their interests. It would be ridiculously naive to accept all or most of the
claims of business apologists about their situation.

On the other hand, it is not clear why the other extreme
position should be accepted: the notion that, whatever businessmen or their mouthpieces said, their behaviour showed they
essentially believed in grabbing everything they could without
getting caught. In some rigid theoretical formulations, of course,
this charge is unanswerable. A dogmatic Marxist position which
holds that all businessmen in a capitalist system are exploitive
and/or immoral is irrefutable because no evidence from within
the system can count against it. It rests on an equation of profit
with the appropriation of surplus labour value so that profits, by
definition, can never be anything but theft. Leaving aside the
unverifiability and dubiousness of this proposition, it is interesting that a moderately sophisticated Marxist would not deny the
sincerity of the business thought outlined in this book. His
concern is with a corrupt system not with the integrity and
morality of individuals acting within the system. A Marxist could
easily accept the idea of a thrifty, industrious, enterprising, solicitous, and dedicated capitalist bourgeoisie, yet still condemn a mode
of production necessarily based on the appropriation of value created by workers.

It is more common, particularly among liberal intellectuals, to
believe that the world of business has been peopled by immoral
individuals, men driven by lust to make money – simple greed –
who in their eagerness for profits have disregarded justice, good
taste, morality, and, as often as possible, the law. This is a more
interesting proposition because it is open to proof or disproof by
the normal use of evidence. Some proof is surely required, for it is
not reasonable to begin with the assumption that a whole occupational group in society is or was characterized by individuals guilty
of sins ranging from hypocrisy to immoral and illegal behaviour.

No historian of Canadian society has yet studied business
reality in the ways that these chapters have examined business
thought. No one has even offered a satisfactory definition of
"exploitation," let alone tried to measure the amount of exploitation of Canadian working people. No one knows enough
about the careers of a large enough number of entrepreneurs to
comment on the means by which most business leaders in Can-

135

ada achieved success. No one knows how many businessmen approached politicians with cash in hand or satchel, or how to measure the relative power exercised by the leaders of the various interest groups in a pluralistic democracy. No one has tried to compare the numbers of dishonest businessmen with the numbers of dishonest workers, farmers, politicians, or historians.

Consider two problems. What would a study of discipline in the home and school in the 1880s tell us, for the sake of comparison, about the discipline in J. M. Fortier's tobacco factory in Montreal? Surely it would suggest that Fortier had his counterparts in classrooms and homes everywhere in the country, that his methods were not a reflection of a new barbarism brought on by industrialism, but rather were based on mores common in a society still characterized, in P. B. Waite's phrase, by "elemental crudeness."[1] Or, if it were possible to design a study to measure the incidence of greed in a society, is it likely that other classes could be shown to be significantly less greedy than men in business? It is surely significant that all of the evidence presented in Chapter 1 is consistent with Max Weber's classic interpretation of *The Protestant Ethic and the Spirit of Capitalism* in which he drew attention to the semi-ascetic characteristics of an economic impulse based on deferred gratification. As for greed or acquisitiveness, Weber argued,

> The impulse to acquisition, pursuit of gain, of money, or of the greatest possible amount of money, has in itself nothing to do with capitalism. This impulse exists and has existed among waiters, physicians, coachmen, artists, prostitutes, dishonest officials, soldiers, nobles, crusaders, gamblers, and beggars. One may say that it has been common to all sorts and conditions of men at all times and in all countries of the earth, wherever the objective possibility of it is or has been given. It should be taught in the kindergarten of cultural history that this naive idea of capitalism must be given up once and for all. Unlimited greed for gain is not in the least identical with capitalism, and is still less its spirit. Capitalism *may* even be identical with the restraint, or at least a rational tempering of this irrational impulse.[2]

In general, the evidence presented here suggests a mixed and complex picture of the relationship of business ideology and practice. Some men in business were extraordinarily money-hungry, others thought profit a by-product of excellence in business. Some beat and kicked their workers, others paid high wages and built baseball diamonds. Some corrupted legislatures, others worked for

civil service reform and honest government. Some formed combines and gouged the public, others combined in the literal hope of
making a living profit. In personal correspondence the occasional
businessman's public rectitude was replaced by privately venality.
More commonly, the private letters were sprinkled with the same
maxims and arguments that were the stuff of the editorials in the
business press. When George Stephen, utterly exasperated with the
government's treatment of the C.P.R., finally reminded Sir John
A. Macdonald in 1890 of the size of his political contributions, he
went right on to say, "I have not asked, and would not ask anything
of the Gov't but what is right & fair, and which ought to be granted
even had I never done a thing or spent a dollar for it politically."[3]
And even when businessmen's views were an obvious distortion of
reality, when, say, the manufacturers decided in 1911 that the
Canadian Government could only be influenced by farmers and
workers, there was no question of the sincerity of ideas expressed in
a private meeting. That ideas are often based on misunderstanding,
self-deception, and self-interest does not lessen their holder's con-
viction or the likelihood that he will base his actions on them.
Indeed, the historian trying to account for irrational behaviour – an
unwarranted flight of capital or a costly and silly resistance to a
moderate trade union – ignores the likelihood of actors being motivated by grossly distorted perceptions of reality only at his peril.

On a number of issues there is no doubt of the inaccuracy of the
convictions held by businessmen. Much of the analysis of trade
unions and the whining about the priorities of governments, to take
only two examples, was clearly absurd, if, nonetheless, understandable. On other issues much more work needs to be done to compare reality with businessmen's perceptions. There is supporting
evidence, for example, to indicate that their complaints about the
educational system, particularly in Quebec, were well-founded.[4] In
their criticisms of "professional politicians" and the party system
businessmen appear to have been reflecting the "revolt against
party government" that Carl Berger has shown to have been common among thoughtful Canadians in the half-century after Confederation.[5] Perhaps future analyses of social and power structures will
support the notions that the liberal professions enjoyed a dispro-
portionate share of social prestige, of legislative privilege, and, at
least in the case of lawyers, of political representation and power.
Businessmen also appear to have been broadly accurate in their
belief that industrial development in the 1880s had been beneficial
to the workingman. All of the individual injustices and specific
grievances uncovered by the Royal Labor Commission should not

obscure its major finding: "that wages in Canada are generally higher than at any previous time, while hours of labor have been somewhat reduced. At the same time, the necessaries and ordinary comforts of life are lower in price than ever before, so that the material conditions of the working people who exercise reasonable prudence and economy have been greatly bettered."[6] Similarly, the reports of factory inspectors, even those drawn from the ranks of trade unionists, tended to support employers' arguments on child labour and the conditions in their factories.[7] What no one testifying before the Royal Labor Commission in the late 1880s seems to have understood was that the real question at issue was not whether old standards of work and wages were being violated, but rather what new and higher expectations and standards should be fulfilled in an age of economic progress.

There will naturally be a continuing debate among Canadian historians on most of these problems. We are especially likely to refight the old battle among English historians as to whether the coming of industrial production raised or lowered the standards of living of the working class. It seems clear at this stage of investigation that most of the ideas current in the business community were in varying degrees grounded in the real world as it appeared to men of affairs, and that businessmen, like most other people, meant what they said. It would not have been necessary to argue these points at all if this book had been about the ideas of workers, farmers, or intellectuals, groups whom most students of Canadian history do not automatically distrust.

In any case, these studies have been only peripherally about the reality of business practice. They have concentrated on the kinds of ideas that men in business happen to have expressed. The most interesting conclusions arising from this material relate not so much to the gap between business practice and business thought as they do to the characteristics and implications of the cast of mind common among businessmen of this period.

When they talked about success in business, or at anything else in life, businessmen were deeply individualistic. They held each man personally responsible for his success or failure in life, and were worried that vital principles of self-discipline and self-help were everywhere threatened by idleness, extravagance, gambling, dissipation, and other vices. There were two contradictory aspects of this anxiety. On the one hand it seemed that most people, particularly workers, were not naturally committed to the success values, that they had to be moulded into suitably self-disciplined, success-oriented ways of behaviour. It seemed that a system of values had to be imposed on a society many members of which had not practised them in the past nor were ordinarily inclined to practise them at any time. In this view Canadian economic development was being held back by a set of attitudes which had to be destroyed – Canadians had still to become a disciplined, success-oriented people.

On the other hand, businessmen feared the corrupting effects of the economic development they were working so strenuously to produce. In a new age of affluence where success might come without effort, all the incentives to self-control and self-improvement would be lost. Gratification would no longer be deferred while capital was accumulated, society would revel in trinkets and amusements, and the syndrome of the rich man's idle son would become general.* This perception was permeated by a sense of an old order passing, an existing social concensus breaking down instead of a new one being formed. To many in business the rise of worker and agrarian collectivism seemed part and parcel of it all, a reflection of individuals' deep desires to avoid responsibility, to get something for nothing, to throw the burden on others' shoulders. It was almost good for society when a downturn in the business cycle brought back a dose of hard times, the old poverty which had done so much to strengthen the moral character of Canadians.

But for most businessmen, individualism, though a prerequisite of business success, was not enough. Even though a man might be hard-working, thrifty, and honest, competition could destroy his livelihood. How could the railway president or the corner grocer protect himself from the forces generated by an open market, a situation offering no security, no certainty, no sense of control over one's own economic fate? Business history will only accurately describe the full consequences of a competitive economic

---

\* Here, too, there may have been a substantial social reality underlying the sometimes comical complaints about the bad effects of wealth. Attempting to explain British industrial stagnation in the late nineteenth century in *The Unbound Prometheus: Technological Change and Industrial Development in Western Europe from 1750 to the Present* (Cambridge: 1969), David S. Landes argues seriously that "prosperity and success are their own worst enemies." Referring to the ambition and enterprise of the first two generations who ran family businesses, Landes goes on: "now it was the turn of the third generation, the children of affluence, tired of the tedium of trade and flushed with the bucolic aspirations of the country gentleman. . . . Many of them retired and forced the conversion of their firms into joint-stock companies. Others stayed on and went through the motions of entrepreneurship between the long weekends; they worked at play and played at work" (p. 336). It is, of course, now common to argue that the material security of an affluent society is diminishing the impulse to hard work and thrift.

system when it stops concentrating on enterprises that succeeded and also takes note of the lists of failures that were the staple of every trade journal and the spectre haunting every businessman hoping to succeed.

The restrictionist movement in Canadian business was a practical response to the insecurities of open competition. Protective tariffs, price-fixing combines, early-closing movements, were all attempts to ease the strain of business life, the insecurity and fear of failure that the *Commercial* once called "dyspepsia of the mind."[8] Economic liberalism was still theoretical orthodoxy, the doctrine everyone had to pay lip service to and a few held as gospel. Restrictionist ideas, which came to dominate business discussions of competition, were the not always thought-out conclusions and arguments that emerged from everyday life in the marketplace. Competition was the life of trade, but ... it was even more important to get a "living profit." The flight from competition in business in the late nineteenth century can best be understood in the framework of the process Karl Polanyi called "the great transformation": the spontaneous and massive counter-movement by all classes in European and North American society in the nineteenth century against the destructive forces of laissez faire and the free market.[9] Being human, most businessmen were no more willing than farmers or workers to engage in a wide-open competitive struggle for economic survival, to be puppets dancing on strings held by the invisible hand.

Most businessmen would have indignantly denied having any less interest in their employees' securing a "living wage" than in themselves making a "living profit." They claimed that Canadian workers were enjoying unprecedented prosperity, that conditions of employment and opportunities for advancement were as good as or better than they had ever been, and that most of a workingman's problems stemmed from his own unwillingness to be thrifty, sober, and hard-working. A number of businessmen did support social reform to protect the helpless worker and did try to keep reasonably up-to-date in the conditions of employment they offered. Where they could not meet worker requests for improvement in wages or working conditions they usually pleaded the unpleasant necessities of competition.

But they drew the line at workingmen combining to insist on a living wage. Here was the glaring contradiction in business thought about competition and its consequences. In business competition was understood to be apt to prevent a man from earning a living profit even though he might be hard-working, thrifty, and honest; combination was a necessary corollary of individualism, the supplementary arrangement to make sure individual effort received a decent reward. This was exactly the argument trade unionists used to justify their organizations: hard-working, thrifty, and honest workers needed organizations to guarantee that their efforts received a decent reward. Businessmen never understood this. Individualism, though clearly insufficient for business success, was deemed perfectly sufficient for success as a worker or farmer. Business was justified in striving mightily to overcome the laws of supply and demand and the forces of the marketplace; others should bend to them. Co-operation was the keynote of the new business philosophy; hard work and saving were to be others' code. The leaders of trade combines were business statesmen; the leaders of labour unions and farmers' organizations were parasitical demagogues. The price-cutter in business was a pirate, reckless and unethical; the scab worker was a free and honest man.

Even in the context of the real competitive world and the requirements of the balance sheet, businessmen could have been conscious of alternatives. They could have recognized labour's legitimate interest in organization and could have explored the possibilities of mutual organization for protection and advancement. The vehicle of the trade association could as easily have been used for worker elevation as it was for price-fixing. In the cotton industry, for example, the various combines could have tried to use their monopoly power to agree on improvements in wages and working conditions, petitioning the government for increased protection to keep out lower-cost foreign goods. Although there were petitions enough for more protection, there is not a trace of evidence in the reports of textile combines indicating that any thought was given to agreements to uplift the factory hands; instead there is only evidence of collusion to lower wages.[10] The Canadian Bankers' Association made only a few token attempts in its early years to take an interest in bank clerks; though almost certainly capable of enforcing higher standards of work and wages, the C.B.A. lapsed into sustained neglect of one of the hardest pressed and most defenceless groups in the labour force.[11] Although the various trade sections of the Canadian Manufacturers' Association could debate for hours on limiting competitive practices amongst their members, only one of the surviving minute books records a single discussion of the possibilities of collective action to improve the lot of workers, and it was not taken.[12] The C.M.A. itself encouraged a collective stand on dozens of issues affecting manufacturers, but refused to endorse the principle of a Saturday half-holiday in manufacturing on the ground that this decision was up to the individual manufacturer.[13] In 1908 the C.M.A. did adopt a constructive course of co-operation with organized labour that produced the model Ontario Workman's Compensation Act of 1915. This was an indication of what might have been, but had come a bit late in the day. As early as the 1880s social welfare programmes such as health insurance and pension plans were being introduced in Europe; no important Canadian businessmen had the imagination to see how labour and capital could co-operate to improve the security of Canadians.[14]

In the United States in the early years of the twentieth century the big businessmen of the National Civic Federation began to develop their vision of "corporate liberalism" or a "business commonwealth" in which oligopolistic capital and business unionism would co-operate for mutual benefit, and they carried these ideas on into the 1920s and the National Reconstruction Administration in the 1930s. In Canada, by contrast, there is little evidence of any similar movement, except perhaps the continuing interest in collectivism on the part of the Retail Merchants' Association, whose remarkable tenacity in advocating its ideas finally achieved momentary recognition in the 1930s with the Stevens Commission and R. B. Bennett's "New Deal."[15] From the point of view of individual liberty and economic efficiency it may have been just as well that collectivism of either the right or the left never substantially flourished in North America. But in terms of the dominant thrust of business behaviour and thought in the late nineteenth and early twentieth centuries, which was towards a self-interested collectivism, the fact that bringing workers into the embryonic system was seldom considered, let alone tried, indicates the *ad hoc* and unimaginative nature of business thought about the "labor question." Their ideas about other people moulded in the categories of individualism, their immediate day-to-day interests precluding a wide-ranging consideration of what was happening in Canadian society, business leaders failed to see the possibilities of labour and capital taking action in their common interest.

A good deal of business thought on other social issues involved a distorted perspective. Political attitudes, for example, were shaped in part by occupational experience. Business predisposed a man to be impatient with factions and pluralism. The practical businessman was used to making his own decisions and seeing them promptly executed. Decisions were made solely according to the narrow interests of the firm; administrative work placed a premium on competence and efficiency. Being "businesslike" meant getting things done fast, competently, and with a minimum of debate. Few businessmen were able to understand why politics could not work on the same principles. Nor could they understand why politicians did not respond instantly to the needs of business. Believing that business enterprise really was fundamental to Canadian national development, believing in fact in the myth of the businessman as social benefactor, they could not understand the failure of the state to give absolute priority to business interests. Even protectionists' success at identifying the tariff with Canadian national development was not enough; the National Policy had to be above politics, part of Canada's "national business principles" before protectionists could breathe easy. The modest responsiveness of governments to other interests on tariff or any other issues appeared to be a reversal of proper priorities, explicable only in terms of the self-interested machinations of unprincipled politicians. Businessmen came to view themselves as a minority interest, underrepresented in and ignored by government. Combining a realization of the fact that business interests would always be outvoted in elections with their absurdly high expectations, businessmen tended, rightly or wrongly, to feel alienated from the political system.

Because there is wide interest in drawing up an historical balance-sheet of the relationship between businessmen and social reform, it bears repeating that businessmen were divided on most issues involving the role of government in Canadian economic life. As a group they reflected no political ideology beyond a belief that it was the function of government to advance the interests of business. Businessmen favoured those "reforms" that advanced their interests, opposed those that did not. On any given issue there were apt to be vested business interests opposing change and "public-spirited" businessmen supporting reform. Unduly emphasizing either part of that statement leads to incorrect generalizations: that businessmen always resisted reform, that business was a force for social progress, or that all reform was illusory because there was business self-interest lurking in the background.

Finally, the quality of social thought in the business community was low. Businessmen tended to interpret the world in stereotypes, half-formed preconceptions based partly on the familiar methods and mores of business life, partly on a tendency to generalize from the worst in other people's behaviour. Their ideas were often crude rationalizations, attempts to put vague and confused emotions into coherent language. As practical men and not "mere theorists," businessmen were not ideologues, yet in their social thought they wrenched complex reality into categories as grossly simplistic as any narrow ideology.

Instead of interpreting these comments as further evidence of failures in social responsibility by businessmen, it might be asked whether the social thought of other occupational groups has been characterized by any greater degree of sophistication. Have spokesmen for other groups – labour, farm interests, even intellectuals – been more successful in overcoming the barriers imposed by particularist experience and self-interest? Are there significant differences, for example, between the rhetoric of businessmen defending combines in the 1890s and that of farm leaders defending "orderly marketing" (a euphemism for agricultural combines), in the 1970s, or between that of businessmen calling on workingmen to be thrifty and hard-working and labour leaders demanding that corporations absorb wage increases through more efficient management? Is it not common in society for members of occupational groups to believe that other occupations are more profitable, in the way that businessmen fantasized about farming? Is what has been called the "homestead psychology" of Canadian businessmen – an instinctive resistance to government interference[17] – a mentality common only to businessmen? Surely educators, trade unionists, and publishers all adopt a stance towards government of welcoming support and subsidies but prophesying catastrophe if government attempts to regulate or control universities, trade unions, or newspapers. It may well be that the ways in which businessmen perceived society and its problems were not particularly unique, but were characteristic of a pattern common to occupational groups struggling to advance their interests in a competitive social order. Much more comparative study of the ideas of spokesmen for other groups is necessary. In the meantime, as an indication of how the rhetoric worked out in practice as industrial society matured, it is worth noting that the restrictive practices of workingmen organized in trade unions, farmers licensed by marketing boards, and professors freed by tenure from the stress of competition are not yet subject to investigation by the Combines Branch.

# Note on Sources

By far the most valuable source for these studies was the editorial and news content of the major Canadian business and trade journals of the period. The *Monetary Times* and the Canadian *Journal of Commerce* were the leading organs of the Toronto and Montreal business communities respectively. In the 1880s a number of more specialized trade journals were founded, including the *Canadian Manufacturer* in 1882, the Winnipeg *Commercial* and *Dominion Dry Goods Report* (shortly the *Canadian Journal of Fabrics*) in 1883, and the *Canadian Grocer* in 1887 by J. B. Maclean. The small French-Canadian business community was served by *Le Moniteur du Commerce* and *Le Prix Courant*, founded in 1880 and 1887 respectively. By the time the Canadian Bankers' Association launched their *Journal* in 1892 they were one of the last major occupational groups of businessmen to have a publication catering to their interests. The two most important newcomers in the first decade of the twentieth century were *Industrial Canada*, founded in 1900 by the Canadian Manufacturers' Association, and the *Financial Post*, the flagship of Maclean's fleet of business papers after 1907.

A few important business publications, notably the Montreal *Shareholder*, the *Canadian Trade Review* (published in Montreal), and most of W. K. McNaught's *Trader*, could not be located and may not be extant. The state of business archives in Canada is still dreadful. A change in the philosophy of trade journal publishing in the late 1890s (shorter paragraphs, simple sentences, less news, and innocuous editorials), combined with the aging of the first generation of crusading and/or verbose editors, meant an abrupt deterioration of such previously excellent trade papers as the Winnipeg *Commercial* and the *Canadian Grocer*. As well, many of the only available runs of a periodical are broken.

Business publications were almost certainly faithful representatives of their readers' opinions. They were self-consciously published in the "interests" of their constituency. Unlike the general press, all of their news and editorial columns were designed to appeal to readers in a specific occupation; circulation and advertising depended on the success of that appeal. Some publications, notably *Industrial Canada* and the *Retail Merchants' Journal* were the house-organs of business organizations and editorially followed a line set by the organization. Many of the smaller trade journals tried to boost circulation by calling themselves the "official" journal of this or that trade association, and tailored their editorial policies accordingly. Some editors were connected with business organizations: James Steen of the *Commercial* served for several years as secretary of the Winnipeg Board of Trade; Stanislas Coté of *Le Moniteur du Commerce* was secretary of La Chambre de Commerce through the 1890s; Frederic Nicholls made the *Canadian Manufacturer* so appealing to manufacturers that he became the OMA-CMA secretary, as was his successor, J. J. Cassidey. Nichols also went on to become a considerable entrepreneur in his own right; so did J. B. Maclean, who turned the *Canadian Grocer* into a publishing empire. All of the business publications encouraged correspondence, printed many articles by and about other businessmen and covered the meetings of trade associations, Boards of Trade, etc. In almost all cases there was no significant variation between attitudes found in editorials and those reported in the news columns.

The evidence collected in two key government investigations of the 1880s – the Royal Commission of the Relations of Capital and Labor and the Select Committee of the House of Commons that investigated combines in 1888 – is even richer in fact and opinion than these limited essays suggest. Other government investigations and reports, notably the annual reports of factory inspectors in Ontario and Quebec, as well as the Parliamentary debates, contain much useful information for the 1890s and 1900s. The seventy volumes of minutes in the archives of the Canadian Manufacturers' Association were an invaluable check on the published activities and opinions of the Association, not least because they show that businessmen were saying in private almost exactly what they were saying in public. A few key collections of businessmen's private papers, especially those of Sir Edmund Walker and Sir Joseph Flavelle, were used to supplement the public sources; major collections of political papers were also sampled and checked on specific issues. Board of Trade reports were not revealing for the purposes of this study, and few of the collections of business records in Canadian archives contain material that is both easily dug out and relevant to the topics considered here.

Secondary sources on which I have directly relied are listed in the text. Excellent bibliographical articles as well as examples of current scholarship in Canadian business history are to be found in David S. Macmillan, ed., *Canadian Business History* (Toronto, 1971), and the Summer 1973 issue of the *Business History Review* (volume XLVII, Number 2). For more complete annotation of the text and a detailed bibliography my original thesis of the same title should be consulted.

# Notes

## Abbreviations Used in the Notes

*C.L.:*      *Canada Lumberman*
*C.G.:*      *Canadian Grocer*
*C.J.F.:*    *Canadian Journal of Fabrics*
*C.M.:*      *Canadian Manufacturer and Industrial World*
*C.M.J.:*    *Canadian Mining Journal*
*C.M.R.:*    *Canadian Mining Review*
*F.P.:*      *Financial Post*
*I.C.:*      *Industrial Canada*
*J.C.:*      *Journal of Commerce*
*J.C.B.A.:*  *Journal of the Canadian Bankers' Association*
*M.C.:*      *Le Moniteur du Commerce*
*M.T.:*      *Monetary Times*
*P.C.:*      *Le Prix Courant*
R.C.L.C.: Royal Commission on the Relations of Labor and Capital in Canada (1889)
*R.M.J.:*    *Retail Merchants' Journal of Canada*
S.C.:      Report of the Select Committee to Investigate and Report Upon Alleged Combinations in Manufactures. Trade and Insurance in Canada. House of Commons, Journals, 1888, Appendix 3.

## Introduction

1. *Dry Goods Review*, May, 1895, p. 6. By contrast see the attempt by T. W. Acheson to establish distinctions in social thought between types of businessmen in chaps. VI and VII of his doctoral thesis, "The Social Origins of Canadian Industrialism: A Study in the Structure of Entrepreneurship" (University of Toronto, 1971) and in his article, "The Social Origins of the Canadian Industrial Elite, 1880-1885," in David S. Macmillan, ed., *Canadian Business History* (Toronto: 1972), pp. 144-74.
2. For the older view see O. D. Skelton, "General Economic History, 1867-1912," Canada and Its Provinces (Toronto: 1914), Vol. IX, chaps. IV and V; W. T. Easterbrook and Hugh G. J. Aitken, *Canadian Economic History* (Toronto: 1956), pp. 395-97. For revisionist suggestions see O. J. Firestone, *Canada's Economic Development, 1867-1953* (London: 1958); Peter B. Waite, *Canada 1874-1896: Arduous Destiny* (Toronto: 1971), pp. 74-77: G. W. Bertram, "Economic Growth in Canadian Industry, 1870-1915: The Staple Model and the Take-off Hypothesis," *Canadian Journal of Economics and Political Science XXIX* (May, 1963), pp. 159-84; Peter J. George and Ernest H. Oksanen, "Recent Developments in the Quantification of Canadian Economic History," *Histoire Sociale/Social History*, No. 4 (Autumn, 1969), pp. 76-92.
3. *Canadian Courier*, Jan. 16, 1909; *Canadian Courier*, Aug. 14, 1909; *Canadian Magazine*, June 11, 1906, p. 6.

4. "To a Millionaire," reprinted in Malcolm Ross, ed., *Poets of the Confederation* (Toronto: 1960), p. 82.

5. F. H. Underhill, "Some Reflections on the Liberal Tradition in Canada," reprinted in *In Search of Canadian Liberalism* (Toronto: 1960), p. 19.

# Chapter 1: Success

1. *C.L.*, Jan., 1906.

2. *J.C.B.A.*, July, 1910, pp. 275-78.

3. *M.T.*, Nov. 8, 1883, p. 512; *M.T.*, Oct. 1, 1897, p. 454; *M.T.*, July 2, 1901, p. 140; *M.T.*, Oct. 5, 1906, p. 455.

4. *J.C.*, Jan. 16, 1891, pp. 117-18; *F.P.*, Feb. 16, 1907; *M.C.*, 7 mai, 1886, p. 317; *C.G.*, Jan. 2, 1894; *Commercial*, Nov. 22, 1897, p. 275; Queen's University, Sir Joseph Flavelle Papers, Flavelle to Borden, Nov. 23, 1909; Alan Wilson, *John Northway, A Blue Serge Canadian* (Toronto: 1965), p. 175; University of Toronto, Sir Edmund Walker Papers, Addresses, File 1, "Y.M.C.A."; *ibid.*, "Address to Schoolmen's Club"; File 2, "Canadian Club, Montreal, 29th January, 1912"; *Globe* letter enclosed in Walker to Rev. J. A. Macdonald, June 29, 1910; Walker to C. W. Kelley, May 1, 1907; Walker to Rev. G. F. Plummer, Aug. 25, 1910.

5. *M.T.*, May 7, 1910, p. 1915.

6. *C.L.*, June, 1906.

7. *F.P.*, May 4, 1907.

8. *M.T.*, Sept. 2, 1891, supplement; *M.T.*, May 7, 1910, p. 1915.

9. J. E. Hansford, *The Business Guide: or, Safe Methods of Business* (Toronto: 1894), p. 8.

10. *M. T.*, June 24, 1881, p. 1510.

11. *M.T.*, Feb. 17, 1905, pp. 1097-98.

12. *J.C.*, Nov. 2, 1906, p. 836.

13. *M.T.*, March 30, 1906, p. 1314; *J.C.*, July 14, 1899, p. 78.

14. *M.C.*, 12 mai, 1886, p. 93.

15. *M.T.*, Dec. 23, 1887, p. 789.

16. *C.G.*, Oct. 6, 1893; R. Laidlaw to Allan Macpherson, June 17, 1902. Professor H. V. Nelles has kindly permitted me to use this quotation from his draft history of the Laidlaw enterprises.

17. *F.P.*, Nov. 16, 1907; *J.C.*, Jan. 3, 1890, p. 23; William Max Aitken, Lord Beaverbrook, *Success* (Toronto: 1921), p. 51.

18. *J.C.*, June 19, 1891, p. 1173.

19. *Commercial*, May 29, 1883, p. 719.

20. *C.M.*, May 15, 1896, p. 422; *F.P.*, Jan. 11, 1908; *F.P.*, Oct. 29, 1910; *F.P.*, Nov. 5, 1910; Public Archives of Canada, Charles Porteous Papers, Vol. 25, p. 5, Porteous to W. A. Campbell, Feb. 26, 1897.

21. *M.T.*, Oct. 27, 1882, p. 459; *J.C.*, Oct. 26, 1883, p. 308.

22. George Hague, *M.T.*, June 30, 1893, p. 1577; *J.C.*, July 1, 1892, p. 18; *M.T.*, Aug. 25, 1893, p. 227; George Cox, *M.T.*, June 10, 1894, p. 1607.

23. Flavelle Papers, Flavelle to J. S. Willison, Oct. 10, 1902.

24. *M.T.*, Aug. 7, 1903, p. 178; *C.M.R.*, 1896-1904, *passim*.

25. *F.P.*, Jan. 9, 1909; Walker Papers, Walker to Frank T. Heffelfinger, July 16, 1908; *F.P.*, Jan. 4, 1908; *C.M.R.*, May, 1901, p. 102.

26. *M.C.* 19 oct., 1900, p. 548; George C. Porter, "James J. Hill, Railroad Magnate," *Busy Man's Magazine*, July 1906; Lord Strathcona, *M.T.*, Oct. 11, 1901, pp. 472-73.

Folder; *M.T.*, Aug. 31, 1883, p. 233; Flavelle Papers, Flavelle to S. J. Moore, Aug. 12; 1903.

27. *J. C.*, June 21, 1889, pp. 1048-49.
28. *M.T.*, May 4, 1906, pp. 1724-25; *J.C.*, Feb. 12, 1904, pp. 453-54.
29. Walker Papers, "Notes for Addresses—Undated" File, "50th Anniversary" Folder; *M.T.*, Aug. 31, 1883, p. 233; Flavelle Papers, Flavelle to S. J. Moore, Aug. 12, 1903.
30. *C.L.*, March, 1906, p. 16; F. H. Clergue, *An Instance of Industrial Evolution in Northern Ontario. An Address by Francis H. Clergue . . . Delivered at a General Meeting of the Board of Trade of the City of Toronto, April 2, 1900* (n.p., n.d.), p. 15; Senate, *Debates,* March 30, 1898, pp. 523-24; William Van Horne, *Busy Man's Magazine,* Dec., 1905, pp. 25-27; *M.T.,* Nov. 24, 1906, p. 738.
31. J. W. Dafoe, *Clifford Sifton in Relation to His Times* (Toronto: 1931), pp. 527, 528.
32. Flavelle Papers, Flavelle to R. J. Cromie, July 19, 1935; *ibid.,* Flavelle to D. Carnegie, Oct. 14, 1922; case 57, speech to the Winnipeg Board of Trade, March 10, 1924.
33. Public Archives of Canada, R. B. Bennett Papers, p. 490588, Bennett to J. G. Bennett, Oct. 21, 1931; Ralph Allen, *Ordeal By Fire* (Toronto: 1961), p. 30.
34. Castell Hopkins and George Denison, quoted in C. C. Berger, *The Sense of Power* (Toronto: 1970), pp. 196, 182.

# Chapter 2: The Flight from Competition

1. S.C., pp. 3-5, 505-7, 526-27.
2. Montreal Board of Trade Archives, Montreal Wholesale Grocers' Association, Minutes, 1888-1891, *passim.*
3. *Ibid.*, Letterbooks, J. S. Cook to Messrs. Walter Baker & Sons, Dec. 14, 1908.
4. *Ibid.*, Minutes, 1900-1915, *passim.*
5. G. R. Stevens, *Canadian National Railways*, Vol. 1 (Toronto: 1960), pp. 347-53; Public Archives of Canada, C.P.R. Papers, Van Horne Letterbooks, No. 5, Van Horne to James Stephenson, April 29, 1884; *ibid.,* No. 6, Van Horne to W. Wainwright, May 22, 1884; *ibid.,* No. 10, *passim.*
6. Walter Vaughan, *The Life and Work of Sir William Van Horne* (New York: 1920), p. 166; C.P.R. Papers, Van Horne Letterbooks, No. 14, Van Horne to G. M. Bosworth, Dec. 8, 1885.
7. *C.M.,* Oct. 19, 1883, p. 764.
8. *Report of the Royal Commission on the Textile Industry* (Ottawa: 1938), p. 119.
9. House of Commons, *Debates,* April 8, 1889, p. 1112.
10. *C.G.,* March 7, 1890.
11. S.C., *passim.*
12. *J.C.B.A.,* Oct., 1895, p. 20; *J.C.B.A.,* Jan., 1900, pp. 97, 98.
13. *P.C.,* 27 déc., 1889; *C.G.,* Oct. 22, 1890.
14. *C.J.F.,* March 1887, pp. 59, 83; *M.T.,* June 1, 1888, p. 1482; *Commercial,* June 18, 1888, p. 996.
15. *Trader,* Oct., 1890, p. 31; *Trader,* Nov., 1900, p. 1.
16. *C.G.,* Feb. 26, 1892; *C.G.,* Nov. 22, 1895.
17. *R.M.J.,* July 20, 1903, p. 12.

18. *Ibid.*, Aug., 1905, p. 255.
19. Public Archives of Ontario, Lumberman's Association of Ontario Papers, transcript of "Special General Meeting of Lumber Manufacturers," May 6, 1908; also, House of Commons, *Journals,* 1906-1907, Appendix 6, "Proceedings of the Select Committee . . . Inquiring into the Prices Charged for Lumber in the Provinces of Manitoba, Alberta and Saskatchewan."
20. *M.T.,* Sept. 24, 1910, pp. 1325-28; *F.P.,* July 30, Sept. 17, Oct. 22, 1910.
21. *R.M.J.,* Aug., 1907, p. 257.
22. *J.C.,* Jan. 19, 1894, p. 135; *J.C.,* July 15, 1887, pp. 66-67; *C.G.,* Nov. 7, 1890.
23. *Trader,* April, 1883; *C.M.*, Aug. 18, 1882, p. 469; *Commercial,* June 23, 1885, p. 769; Public Archives of Canada, The Royal Commission on Railways, "Evidence," *passim; I.C.*, Oct. 1903, p. 117.
24. *Trader,* March, 1890, p. 23.
25. Public Archives of Canada, Laurier Papers, pp. 111449-53, W. K. McNaught to Laurier, June 22, 1906.
26. S.C., pp. 19-25, 88-89, 113; Montreal Wholesale Grocers' Association, Minutes, Nov. 17, 1893.
27. S.C., pp. 84-85.
28. *C.G.,* Dec. 12, 1890; *C.G.,* Oct. 17, 1890; *C.G.,* May 15, 1891.
29. S.C., pp. 29-32; Laurier Papers, p. 5770, J. A. Mathewson to Laurier, July 20, 1896; T. Eaton Co., *Spring and Summer Catalogue, 1894,* p. 3; Public Archives of Canada, R. L. Borden Papers, Joseph Flavelle to Borden, Feb. 21, 1910; Senate, *Debates,* May 2, 1910, pp. 886-88; *M.T.* May 7, 1910, p. 1915.
30. *C.J.F.,* April 1896, p. 100.
31. *C.G.,* May 17, 1889; *M.T.,* Dec. 10, 1886, p. 664; *Commercial,* March 15, 1887, p. 510.
32. *C.G.,* April 11, 1889, *J.C.,* Aug. 20, 1889, p. 529.
33. S.C., pp. 122-24; W. J. Ashley, "The Canadian Sugar Combine," *University Quarterly Review* 1 (Feb., 1890), 38; *M.T.*, Aug 23, 1889, p. 223.
34. S.C., p. 110; *R.M.J.*, Oct. 20, 1903, p. 73; *P.C.*, 8 mai, 1894, pp. 272-73.
35. *C.G.*, Oct. 2, 1891; *C.J.F.*, April, 1886, p. 186; D. M. Stewart, "What Constitutes Unwise Competition Between Banks," *J.C.B.A.*, Jan., 1898, p. 223.
36. *C.M.,* Sept. 28, 1883, p. 703.
37. S.C., pp. 88, 355; "Select Committee on Lumber, 1907," pp. 655-57.
38. *M.T.,* May 25, 1888, p. 1448.
39. "Select Committee on Lumber, 1907," pp. 601, 602.
40. S.C., pp. 45-46.
41. *M.T.,* Sept. 24, 1910, p. 1327.
42. Hugh Blain, *Combines: An Address Delivered Before the Board of Trade of the City of Toronto by Mr. Hugh Blain Against the Bill Introduced in the House of Commons by Mr. N. Clarke Wallace Intitled "An Act For the Prevention and Suppression of Combinations in Restraint Trade."* (Toronto: 1889), pp. 11-12; "Select Committee on Lumber, 1907," p. 657.
43. Blain, *op. cit.;* Stelco, *M.T.,* Sept. 24, 1910, pp. 1326-27; see also Herbert Gordon Stapells, "The Recent Consolidation Movement in Canadian Industry," (M.A. Thesis, University of Toronto, 1922).
44. *R.M.J.,* Dec., 1906, p. 389.
45. *Ibid.,* May, 1904, p. 91; Ashley, *op. cit.,* p. 38.
46. *M.T.,* April 5, 1889, p. 1185.
47. *C.G.,* July 10, 1891; *C.G.,* Dec. 4, 1896.
48. *R.M.J.,* Aug. 20, 1903, pp. 48-49; *Canadian Pharmaceutical Journal,*

March, 1897, p. 313; *M.C.*, 6 août, 1886, p. 548; T. J. Drummond, *I.C.*, Nov., 1909, p. 428.

49. *Commercial*, Sept. 16, 1889, p. 1269; "Select Committee on Lumber, 1907," pp. 238, 278; David R. Forgan, "Banking as a Profession," *J.C.B.A.*, Oct., 1898, p. 52.

50. *J.C.*, Aug. 20, 1886, p. 529; *C.M.*, March 15, 1889, p. 178; Senate, *Debates*, April 29, 1889, pp. 643, 650; *I.C.*, May, 1910, p. 978.

51. *C.G.*, Feb. 26, 1892, p. 26.

52. Bliss, *op. cit.*

# Chapter 3: The Workingman's Welfare

1. R.C.L.C., *Report*, p. 10.

2. *Ibid., Quebec Evidence*, pp. 94-104, 123-32, 207-9, 388-90.

3. *C.M.*, Oct. 4, 1889, p. 226; also, R.C.L.C., *Ontario Evidence*, pp. 897-98; *ibid., Quebec Evidence*, p. 377.

4. Canadian Manufacturers' Association Archives, Toronto Branch Executive, Minutes, March 14, 1907; R.C.L.C., *Nova Scotia Evidence*, p. 294; Public Archives of Canada, W. L. M. King Papers, Royal Commission Respecting Industrial Disputes in the Province of Quebec (1907), Minutes of Evidence, p. 1068.

5. R.C.L.C., *Quebec Evidence*, pp. 394, 397.

6. Royal Commission on Cotton Factories, Minutes, p. 1010; the annual reports of the factory inspectors are printed as a separate paper in the Ontario *Sessional Papers* from 1889, as part of the Report of the Commissioner of Agriculture and Colonization in the Quebec *Sessional Papers*, 1890-92, thereafter as part of the Report of the Commissioner of Public Works, and as an appendix to the *Journals and Proceedings of the House of Assembly of Nova Scotia* from 1909.

7. C.M.A., Toronto Branch Executive, Minutes, March 14, 1907.

8. R.C.L.C., *Quebec Evidence*, pp. 1310, 1177.

9. *Ibid., Ontario Evidence*, p. 553; *ibid., Quebec Evidence*, p. 161; E. T. Corkill, "Mine Accidents," *Journal of the Canadian Mining Institute*, 12 (1909), pp. 324-42.

10. R.C.L.C., *Ontario Evidence*, p. 296.

11. *Ibid.*, pp. 897-98; *ibid., Nova Scotia Evidence*, p. 279; Royal Commission on Cotton Factories, Minutes, p. 1008; factory inspectors' reports, *passim*.

12. Canada, *Sessional Papers*, 1882, No. 42, "Report of the Commissioners appointed to inquire into the working of Mills and Factories of the Dominion, and the labor employed therein," p. 7.

13. David Morrice, R.C.L.C., *Quebec Evidence*, p. 381; Frederic Nicholls, R.C.L.C., *Ontario Evidence*, p. 190; House of Commons, *Debates*, Feb. 6, 1907, p. 2615; *M.T.*, Feb. 12, 1886, p. 1011; C.M.A., Executive Council, Minutes, Feb. 21, 1907.

14. *C.M.*, Aug. 19, 1887, p. 119; *M.T.*, July 13, 1900, p. 53; *J.C.*, March 3, 1893, p. 331; *M.C.* 9 mai, 1890, p. 446.

15. R.C.L.C., *Nova Scotia Evidence*, p. 417.

16. George Hague, *Some Practical Considerations on the Subject of Capital and Labor, With the Bearing of Christianity on the Subject* (Montreal: 1894), *passim*.

17. *J.C.*, Nov. 23, 1883, p. 440; *J.C.*, Dec. 3, 1886, p. 1549.

18. *M.T.*, May 16, 1890, p. 1417.

19. *I.C.*, July 1903, p. 525; *J.C.*, Feb. 5, 1892, p. 241.
20. *M.T.*, June 10, 1898, p. 1610; *C.M.*, Dec. 20, 1889, p. 405; *C.M.*, Feb. 3, 1888, p. 81; *C.M.*, Nov. 12, 1897, pp. 417-18; *C.M.*, May 4, 1888, p. 296; *C.M.*, Jan 3, 1896, p. 16; *M.C.*, 17 fév., 1888, p. 11.
21. *M.T.*, June 2, 1882, p. 1479; *C.M.*, Feb. 17, 1882, p. 51; *C.M.*, March 15, 1889, p. 178; C.M.A., General Minute Book 1886-1899, "Minutes of a meeting of manufacturers . . . 30th day of November 1886 for the purpose of discussing the probable effect that recent labor legislation would have on native industry."
22. R.C.L.C., *Quebec Evidence*, pp. 536-37; *ibid., Ontario Evidence*, pp. 744-45, 811; *ibid., Quebec Evidence*, p. 807.
23. *M.T.*, Jan. 6, 1882, p. 818; *C.M.*, July 28, 1882, p. 385; *C.J.F.*, Jan., 1888, p.28; Laurier Papers, pp. 29009-10, John Waldie to Laurier, Dec. 27, 1898; *C.L.*, Aug. 15, 1910, p. 38.
24. *M.T.*, Dec. 3, 1880, pp. 640-41; *C.M.*, May 12, 1882, p. 170; *C.M.*, May 2, 1890, p. 304; *M.T.*, Nov. 23, 1889, p. 618; *C.J.F.*, Dec., 1897, pp. 367-71; on company towns see R.C.L.C., *Nova Scotia Evidence*, p. 408 ff.; *ibid., New Brunswick Evidence*, pp. 444-68; *ibid., Quebec Evidence*, pp. 1247-63; also *C.J.F.*, Dec., 1897, pp. 367-71; *M.T.*, May 30, 1890, p. 1486.
25. *I.C.*, 1907-1910, *passim*; especially, "Industrial Betterment in Canadian Factories," Jan., 1907, p. 506; Thomas Roden, "The Housing of Workmen," March, 1907, pp. 653-54; Helen Sterling, "Welfare Work and Factories," Nov., 1909, pp. 424-27.
26. *Canadian Annual Review, 1913*, pp. 722-24; C.M.A., Toronto Branch Executive, Minutes, June 14, Nov. 8, 1906; *ibid.*, May 14, June 13, Dec. 13, 1907; *ibid.*, Oct. 14, 1909; *ibid.*, May 12, 1910; *ibid.*, Jan. 30, Dec. 13, 1911.
27. Murray G. Ross, *The Y.M.C.A. in Canada: The Chronicle of a Century* (Toronto: 1951), pp. 122-26, 234-37; A. E. Fitzpatrick, "Social Amelioration in the Lumber Camps," *C.L.*, May, 1904.
28. *Report of the Royal Commission on Industrial Disputes in British Columbia* (Ottawa: 1903), p. 789; *C.J.F.*, March, 1893, p. 65.
29. *I.C.*, Jan., 1908, p. 496; on the C.M.A.'s campaign for technical education, see Robert Stamp, "Technical Education, the National Policy, and Federal-Provincial Relations in Canadian Education, 1899-1919," *Canadian Historical Review* 52, No. 4 (Dec., 1971): 404-423.
30. C.M.A., Toronto Branch Executive, Minutes, Nov. 8, 1906; *ibid.*, May 13, July 8, 1909.
31. *I.C.*, Nov., 1909, p. 424.
32. *J.C.*, Aug. 15, 1890, p. 737; *M.T.*, Aug. 7, 1885, p. 156; *J.C.*, Sept. 7, 1888, p. 452.
33. *C.M.*, Oct. 5, 1888, p. 240; *I.C.*, April, 1910, p. 868.

# Chapter 4: Unions

1. *Royal Commission on Industrial Disputes in British Columbia*, pp. 687, 192, 294-302.
2. *C.M.J.*, April 15, 1907, p. 92; *C.M.J.*, June 1, 1907, p. 185.
3. *M.T.*, Jan. 3, 1896, p. 852; *Commercial*, April 13, 1886, p. 592; *Commercial*, March 23, 1886, pp. 532-33; *Commercial*, Sept. 9, 1889, p. 1245.
4. *M.T.*, Nov. 7, 1902, p. 592; *C.M.*, Oct. 20, 1893, pp. 313-14; *M.T.*, Sept. 17, 1897, p. 373; *J.C.*, July 15, 1892, p. 103.
5. *P.C.*, 12 mai, 1893; *M.T.*, May 13, 1892, p. 1367; *M.T.*, Nov. 2, 1893, p.

412; *M.T.*, Oct. 10, 1905, p. 595; *J.C.* Oct. 5, 1888, p. 644; *C.M.J.*, April 15, 1910, p. 226.

6. `*I.C.*, April 1909, p. 747.
7. *Trader,* May, 1882; *M.T.*, Oct. 16, 1885, p. 432.
8. *Commercial*, Dec. 18, 1883, p. 228.
9. *J.C.*, Dec. 8, 1893, pp. 1092-93; *I.C.*, Dec., 1907, p. 407.
10. *C.M.*, May 17, 1889, p. 320.
11. *Trader*, May, 1882.
12. *M.T.*, Feb. 12, 1886, p. 1012.
13. *J.C.*, March 13, 1891, p. 502.
14. *I.C.*, April, 1910, p. 891; *M.T.*, Nov. 26, 1889, p. 609; *M.T.*, Aug. 15, 1902, pp. 207-8.
15. *C.M.*, Aug. 17, 1894, pp. 150-51.
16. *I.C.*, July, 1908, p. 1107.
17. *M.T.,* Aug. 27, 1892, p. 214; *J.C.,* July 15, 1902, p. 103; *J.C.,* Nov. 2, 1900, pp. 1194-95.
18. *M.C.*, 29 mai, 1903, p. 694; *J.C.*, Dec. 8, 1893, pp. 1092-93.
19. *M.C.*, 2 nov., 1900, p. 642.
20. *M.T.*, Sept. 15, 1905, p. 330; *C.M.*, Sept. 31, 1887, p. 185; *J.C.*, Oct. 16, 1891, p. 709.
21. *M.T.,* March 16, 1903, p. 1298, referring to a strike in the Crow's Nest Coal Mines.
22. *F.P.*, May 7, 1910, general superintendent of the Nova Scotia Steel and Coal Company to the annual meeting.
23. *M.C.*, 15 mai, 1903, p. 614; *Royal Commission on Industrial Disputes in British Columbia*, pp. 57, 68, 75; *I.C.*, Sept., 1908, p. 90; *J.C.*, July 29, 1910, p. 159.
24. *Canadian Annual Review, 1909,* p. 299.
25. *C.M.J.*, Jan. 1, 1910, p. 14; *C.M.J.*, Aug. 1, 1909, p. 473; *C.M.J.*, Aug. 15, 1909, p. 504; *C.M.J.*, May 1, 1910, p. 281; *C.M.J.*, Sept. 1, 1909, p. 537, *C.M.J.*, Sept. 1, 1909, p. 537.
26. *I.C.*, Aug., 1903, p. 14.
27. Senate, *Debates*, March 20, 1907, p. 515; also, Royal Commission on Cotton Factories, Minutes, pp. 878-82, 1083-89.
28. *F.P.*, Aug. 19, 1911.
29. *C.M.*, March 16, 1888, p. 193.
30. R.C.L.C., *Ontario Evidence,* p. 332; *M.T.*, Sept. 18, 1903, p. 170; *C.M.*, Sept. 6, 1889, p. 149.
31. *M.T.*, Nov. 4, 1898, p. 599; *M.T.*, March 12, 1886, p. 1040.
32. *Royal Commission on Industrial Disputes in British Columbia,* pp. 240, 379-80.
33. *I.C.,* Dec., 1907, p. 407.
34. *C.M.*, Jan. 27, 1893, p. 37; also *C.M.*, Oct. 22, 1892, p. 189; *C.M.*, Feb. 16, 1894, p. 135.
35. R.C.L.C., *Ontario Evidence,* p. 750; *J.C.*, Feb. 5, 1892, p. 241.
36. *C.M.*, July 28, 1882, p. 385; *I.C.*, May, 1909, p. 839.
37. *I.C.*, March, 1908, p. 630.
38. *Royal Commission on Industrial Disputes in British Columbia,* p. 791.
39. *F.P.*, Aug. 20, 1910.
40. *J.C.*, Oct. 16, 1890, p. 737.
41. See, for example, Patricia. Roy, "The British Columbia Electric Railway and Its Street Railway Employees: Paternalism in Labor Relations," *BC Studies*, No. 16 (Winter, 1972-73), pp. 3-24.
42. *C.M.*, March 2, 1886, p. 150; *M.T.*, Oct. 19, 1900, p. 504.

43. *I.C.*, Dec., 1904, pp. 326-27; *M.C.*, 20 août, 1886, pp. 10-11.
44. *I.C.*, Oct., 1903, p. 131; C.M.A., Executive Council, Minutes, March 18, 1909.
45. *I.C.*, Nov., 1905, p. 262.
46. *C.M.*, May 28, 1886, p. 291.
47. *Ibid.*, Jan. 20, 1888, p. 42.
48. *M.T.*, Sept. 26, 1903, p. 388; *I.C.*, Sept., 1904, p. 90.
49. *M.T.*, April 10, 1903, p. 1381; *I.C.*, Oct. 1908, p. 225.
50. C.M.A., Executive Council, Minutes, Sept. 18, 1902.
51. *Ibid.*, Cloak Manufacturers' Section, Minutes, June 5, 1905; *ibid.*, May 31, 1907; Gold and Silversmiths' Section, Minutes, June 5, 1905; Montreal Board of Trade Archives, Montreal Shoe and Leather Association, Minutes, *passim.*
52. *I.C.*, Sept., 1904, p. 99; *I.C.*, Nov., 1907, p. 342; *J.C.*, Dec. 4, 1885, pp. 1150-51.

# Chapter 5: Business, Protection and Nationalism

1. *C.M.*, May 1, 1896, p. 373; *J.C.*, April 7, 1905, p. 860; Public Archives of Canada, Fielding Tariff Inquiry Commission Papers, Vol. 16, p. 997, David Grant to Fielding, May 14, 1904.
2. *Trader*, March, 1880; Senate, *Debates*, March 29, 1897, p. 8.
3. F.T.I.C. Papers, Vol. 11, p. 56, Beethoven Piano Co. to Paterson, April 26, 1902; *ibid.*, Vol. 11, pp. 185-87, N. W. Rowell to Fielding, Feb. 18, 1901.
4. *I.C.*, Nov. 20, 1900, p. 108.
5. C.M.A., Canadian Industrial League, Scrapbook, "To the Point, What a Workingman Thinks of the N.P." (1887).
6. *Ibid.*, "Wages and Work, the Workingman's Interest in the National Policy" (1887).
7. *C.M.*, Nov. 19, 1886, p. 675; F.T.I.C. Papers, Vol. 13, pp. 672-73, Merchants' Cotton Co. to Fielding, Feb. 8, 1902; *I.C.*, Feb., 1911, p. 665.
8. *I.C.*, April, 1911, p. 963.
9. *C.M.*, Sept. 5, 1890, p. 152.
10. *I.C.*, Aug., 1903, p. 10.
11. *C.M.*, Nov. 18, 1892, p. 296; *C.M.*, April 17, 1896, pp. 323-24.
12. Craufurd D. Goodwin, *Canadian Economic Thought, The Political Economy of a Developing Nation* (Durham: 1961), pp. 43-59, 69.
13. *C.M.*, Jan. 6, 1893, p. 3; *I.C.*, Oct., 1903, p. 141; *I.C.*, Feb., 1905, p. 419.
14. Goodwin, *op. cit.*, pp. 43-59.
15. R. C. Brown, *Canada's National Policy, 1883-1900* (Princeton; 1964), pp. 222-32.
16. *I.C.*, Nov., 1903; p. 214, *I.C.*, Dec., 1903, pp. 282-83.
17. *Ibid.*, Oct. 1903, p. 89; *Dry Goods Review*, Feb., 1896, p. 28.
18. *I.C.*, Oct., 1904, p. 122.
19. House of Commons, *Debates*, March 7, 1878, p. 859; *I.C.*, Oct., 1903, p. 154; *I.C.*, Feb., 1902, p. 215.
20. *I.C.*, April, 1909, p. 878; *I.C.*, Oct., 1903, p. 102; *C.M.*, Feb. 1, 1895, p. 115.
21. *I.C.*, Jan., 1904, p. 313; *I.C.*, March, 1909, p. 492; *I.C.*, Dec., 1907, p. 409.
22. *I.C.*, July, 1906, p. 801; *I.C.*, July 1907, p. 917; *I.C.*, March 1910, p. 767.
23. H. V. Nelles, "Empire Ontario: The Problems of Resource Development," in Donald Swainson, ed., *Oliver Mowat's Ontario* (Toronto: 1972), pp. 189-210: O. W. Main, *The Canadian Nickel Industry* (Toronto: 1955); H. G. J. Aitken, ed., *The American Economic Impact on Canada* (Durham: 1959).

24. *C.M.,* March 1, 1895, pp. 201, 207; *I.C.,* March, 1903, p. 362; *I.C.,* Oct., 1903, p. 155.
25. F.T.I.C. Papers, Vol. 12, p. 3, Agricultural Implement Section of the C.M.A. to Laurier, March 30, 1904.
26. B. E. Walker, *I.C.,* Feb., 1911, p. 747; *I.C.,* March 1911, p. 763.
27. *C.M.,* June 15, 1894, p. 500; *C.M.,* April 15, 1888, p. 12; *I.C.,* Feb., 1903, p. 323.
28. C.M.A., Executive Council, Minutes, July 20, 1911; *C.M.,* May 4, 1883, p. 426.
29. *I.C.,* Oct., 1902, p. 163; *I.C.,* June, 1903, pp. 483-84; *C.M.* Feb. 17, 1888, p. 114.
30. *C.M.,* Sept. 5, 1890, p. 158; *C.M.,* Jan. 6, 1893, p. 18; *C.M.,* Jan. 20, p. 48.
31. *C.M.,* May 6, 1887, p. 263; *C.M.,* April 17, 1891, p. 198; *C.M.,* June 5, 1896, p. 468.
32. Bliss, "Canadianizing American Business"; Myra Wilkins, *The Emergence of Multi-National Enterprise* (Cambridge, Mass: 1970), chap. IV.
33. *C.M.,* July 7, 1893, p. 9; *J. C.,* Sept. 30, 1904, p. 700; *M.T.,* March 26, 1897, p. 1278; *M.T.,* Aug. 22, 1902, pp. 241-42.
34. *C.M.,* Jan. 16, 1891, p. 44; *C.M.,* July 4, 1890, p. 9; also *I.C.,* Feb., 1908, p. 543.
35. *C.M.,* June 9, 1882, p. 213 and Feb. 4, 1887, p. 67 for descriptions of Red Parlor meetings; Public Archives of Canada, J. E. Clarke Papers, undated invitation written in Macdonald's hand.
36. Public Archives of Canada, Macdonald Papers, pp. 12440-41, George Stephen to Macdonald, July 29, 1890.
37. *C.M.,* Oct. 19, 1900, p. 12; C.M.A., Executive Council, Minutes, 1910-1912, *passim.*
38. *I.C.,* Oct., 1907, p. 249; *C.M.,* Jan. 1, 1892, p. 9.
39. *C.M.,* July 2, 1897, p. 20.

# Chapter 6: Businessmen and the Community

1. *C.M.,* May 15, 1896, p. 426.
2. *J.C.,* March 17, 1893, p. 417; B. E. Walker, *M.T.,* June 21, 1898, p. 1691; D. R. Wilkie, *J.C.,* Nov. 4, 1898, pp. 634-35; *J.C.,* April 25, 1902, pp. 2062-63; *I.C.,* March, 1906, p. 484.
3. *Commercial,* Nov. 9, 1896, p. 198.
4. *M. C.,* 30 nov., 1883, p. 450; *M. C.,* 7 déc., 1883, p. 476; *M. C.,* 13 avril, 1893, pp. 411-12. For English-Canadian encouragement of agriculture, see almost any issue of the *Commercial,* or, typically, *M. T.,* Dec. 18, 1903, pp. 778-79.
5. *M.C.,* 21 avril, 1899, p. 549; *M.C.,* 6 mars, 1898, p. 593.
6. *J.C.,* Aug. 11, 1893, pp. 264-65; *Commercial,* Sept. 21, 1891, p. 1299.
7. *J.C.,* Dec. 2, 1881, p. 537.
8. *M.T.,* Nov. 23, 1907, p. 827.
9. *C.M.,* March 20, 1891, pp. 187-88.
10. *M.T.,* Feb. 8, 1889, p. 909; *I.C.,* Sept. 20, 1900, p. 64; Royal Commission on Industrial Training and Technical Education, *Report of the Commissioners* (Ottawa; 1913). Part IV, p. 2102.
11. D. R. Wilkie, *J. C.,* Nov. 4, 1898, pp. 634-35; *Dry Goods Review,* Jan., 1896, p. 6; *J.C.,* Nov. 6, 1891, p. 854; *C.M.,* Nov. 17, 1893, pp. 402-3.
12. *M.C.,* 12 déc., 1890, p. 696.
13. *Ibid.,* 11 nov., 1892, p. 560; *ibid.,* 17 août, 1888, pp. 11-12; *ibid.,* 21 oct., 1892, p. 439.

14. *M.T.*, Aug. 11, 1882, p. 151; *J.C.*, Sept. 7, 1888, p. 151.
15. *I.C.*, Oct., 1903, p. 130.
16. *Ibid.*, Oct., 1906, p. 211.
17. *J.C.*, Dec. 6, 1889, p. 990; *F.P.*, Dec. 18, 1909; C.M.A., Tariff Committee, Minutes, Dec. 5, 1890; C.M.A. Executive Council, Minutes, July 20, May 5, 1911.
18. Walker Papers, Walker to Frederick Hamilton, July 29, 1910; *J.C.*, April 13, 1894, pp. 757-58.
19. *M.T.*, Oct. 12, 1894, p. 578; *J.C.*, March 13, 1891, p. 503; *M.T.*, Jan. 23, 1891, pp. 901-2.
20. *M.T.*, Feb. 13, 1891, p. 993.
21. C.M.A., Toronto Branch Executive, Minutes, June 13, 1907; *C.M.J.*, Sept. 1, 1909, p. 514.
22. *C.M.*, Jan. 3, 1896, p. 11; also *J.C.*, Jan. 10, 1896, pp. 64-65; *C.G.*, April 3, 1896, p. 13.
23. *J.C.*, May 23, 1890, pp. 978-80.
24. *Dry Goods Review*, Jan., 1899, p. 76.
25. *C.G.*, June 19, 1896, p. 15.
26. *Ibid.*
27. *Dry Goods Review*, May, 1898, p. 27; *M.C.*, 21 sept., 1900, p. 356.
28. *Commercial,*, Dec. 11, 1893, p. 294; *J.C.*, Aug. 4, 1911, p. 148.
29. *J.C.*, Jan. 1, 1892, pp. 21-22; *M.T.*, Dec. 9, 1898, p. 773.
30. *Commercial*, May 8, 1893, p. 941; *C.G.*, May 24, 1895, p. 15; *C.M.*, July 17, 1896, p. 56; *I.C.*, Oct., 1903, p. 142; Thomas Fyshe, "The Organization of Labor," *J.C.B.A.* (Oct., 1907), pp. 68-86.
31. *C.M.*, June 19, 1896, p. 512; *C.M.*, July 3, 1896, p. 16; E. B. Kirby, "The Influence of Government Upon Mining," *C.M.R.* (Sept., 1902), p. 237; B.C.E.R. quote from Patricia Roy, "The Fine Arts of Lobbying and Persuading; The Case of the B.C. Electric Railway," in David S. Macmillan, ed., *Canadian Business History* (Toronto: 1972), pp. 239-54.
32. Royal Commission on Railways, 1886, Evidence, *passim*.
33. *I.C.*, Oct., 1908, p. 272; *Canadian Annual Review, 1905*, pp. 155-63.
34. *M.T.*, March 25, 1898, p. 1260; *M.T.*, April 1, p. 1306; *M.T.*, June 24, p. 1629; *M.T.*, Jan. 18, 1901, p. 924.
35. C.M.A., Toronto Branch Executive; Minutes, July 10, 1903, W. P. Gundy to the annual meeting; for an exhaustive discussion of the public power movement, see Henry Vivian Nelles, "The Politics of Development: Forests, Mines and Hydro-Electric Power in Ontario, 1890-1939," (Ph.D. Thesis, University of Toronto, 1969), pp. 392-482.
36. *I.C.*, Aug., 1909, p. 36.
37. *Ibid.*, Nov., 1908, pp. 369-70, *et. seq.*
38. *C.M.*, May 4, 1888, p. 302.
39. Macdonald Papers, pp. 95490-93, Joseph Hickson to Macdonald, June 19, 1886; *ibid.*, pp. 123908-9, Stephen to Macdonald, April 21, 1888.
40. C.M.A., Executive Council, Minutes, Jan. 16, 1908.
41. Kirby, *op. cit.*, p. 237; *J.C.*, Nov. 23, 1900, p. 1383.
42. Christopher Armstrong and H. V. Nelles, "Private Property in Peril: Ontario Businessmen and the Federal System, 1898-1911," *Business History Review*, 47, No. 2 (Summer, 1973), pp. 158-76.
43. *Commercial*, Oct. 6, 1885, pp. 28-29, 37.

# Conclusion

1. Peter B. Waite, *Canada 1874-1896: Arduous Destiny* (Toronto: 1971), p. 3.
2. Max Weber, *The Protestant Ethic and the Spirit of Capitalism,* Talcott Parsons, trans. (New York: 1958, orig. pub. 1905), p. 17.
3. Macdonald Papers, pp. 12440-41, Stephen to Macdonald, July 29, 1890.
4. William F. Ryan, *The Clergy and Economic Growth in Quebec, (1896-1914)* (Quebec: 1966), pp. 224, 256, 289-95.
5. Berger, *op. cit.*, pp. 199-210.
6. R.C.L.C., *Report*, p. 8.
7. See the annual reports of factory inspectors as identified in note 6 to Chapter 3, especially those of Robert Hungerford, a trade unionist who was appointed to the Ontario inspectorate in 1908 over very strong objections from the C.M.A. and who confirms virtually all of the opinions of other inspectors.
8. *Commercial*, July 31, 1883, p. 928.
9. Karl Polanyi, *The Great Transformation: The Political and Economic Origins of Our Time* (Boston: 1944).
10. Royal Commission on Cotton Factories, Minutes, pp. 976-77.
11. For a muckraking account of work in Canadian banks before World War I see, J. P. Buschlen, *A Canadian Bankclerk* (Toronto: 1913).
12. C.M.A., Gold and Silversmiths' Section, Minutes, Jan. 29, 1910.
13. *Ibid.*, Executive Council, Minutes, Dec. 20, 1906.
14. *I.C.*, Oct., 1908, p. 226; *I.C.*, July, 1911, p. 1288; for typical business comment on Bismarck's social programme in Germany see *J.C.*, Jan. 13, 1888, pp. 68-69; *J.C.*, Dec. 7, 1888, p. 1078; *J.C.*, May 2, 1890, p. 832.
15. James Weinstein, *The Corporate Ideal in the Liberal State, 1900-1918* (Boston; 1968), chap. 1; Ellis W. Hawley, *The New Deal and the Problem of Monopoly* (Princeton; 1966), pp. 6-11; L.M. Grayson and Michael Bliss, eds., *The Wretched of Canada: Letters to R. B. Bennett, 1930-1935* (Toronto; 1971), Introduction, pp. xvii-xx.
16. V. Nelles and Abraham Rotstein, "Canadian Business and the Eternal No," *Canadian Forum* (January-February, 1972), pp. 61-64.

# Index